D1860070

RULERS OF INDIA

Owing to the antiquity and rarity of this book, certain pages are regrettably absent, and readability is compromised due to the blurring of the original text. If you possess any insights regarding the availability of these missing sections, kindly inform us. Your assistance is crucial in ensuring the completion of this significant work for the benefit of future generations.

RULERS OF INDIA

Viscount Hardinge

AND THE ADVANCE OF THE BRITISH DOMINIONS INTO THE PUNJAB

BY HIS SON AND PRIVATE SECRETARY IN INDIA

CHARLES, SECOND VISCOUNT HARDINGE, B.A.

GYAN

Published by

GYAN

Gyan Publishing House
5, Ansari Road
Daryaganj, New Delhi-110002
Phone: 011-47034999, 9811692060
E-mail: books@gyanbooks.com

Distribution Network
gyanbooks.com
India, USA, Canada, UK, Australia

© Publisher

All rights reserved. No part of this work may be reproduced, stored, adapted, or transmitted in any form or by any means, electronic, mechanical, photocopying, micro-filming, recording or otherwise, or translated in any language, without the prior written permission of the copyright owner and the publisher.

ISBN: 978-81-212-4922-5 (HB)
First Published, 1900

2nd Impression 2024

Printed at: Gyan Press, Delhi.

The book is sold subject to the condition that it shall not, by way of trade or otherwise, be lent, resold, hired out, or otherwise circulated without the prior publisher's written consent.

RULERS OF INDIA
Author: CHARLES, SECOND VISCOUNT HARDINGE

Rulers of India

RULERS OF INDIA

Viscount Hardinge

BY HIS SON AND PRIVATE SECRETARY IN INDIA

CHARLES VISCOUNT HARDINGE, B.A.

Oxford

AT THE CLARENDON PRESS: 1900

Dedicated by Permission

To the Queen

and

Empress of India

PREFACE

The following pages are a simple narrative of the principal incidents in the career of one of the 'Rulers of India,' a career marked by eventful scenes in both European and Oriental history. The narrative is based on public documents, family papers, and letters of Lord Hardinge, written immediately after the events they describe—some of them almost on the field of battle. I have ventured to add some personal recollections of the period when I was his Private Secretary in India. But I feel that the words which his own pen indited portray his character better than descriptions and arguments by another hand. It has been my special aim to throw light upon those matters to which my Father himself attached importance, and concerning which his desire was that they should, after due lapse of time, become publicly known.

With regard to the literary arrangement of the work, I have to acknowledge the assistance of Mr. J. S. Cotton, which has been of great value.

HARDINGE.

South Park, Penshurst,
March, 1891.

CONTENTS

NOTE

The orthography of proper names follows the system adopted by the Indian Government for the *Imperial Gazetteer of India*. That system, while adhering to the popular spelling of very well-known places, such as Punjab, Lucknow, &c., employs in all other cases the vowels with the following uniform sounds:—

a, as in wom*a*n : *á*, as in l*a*nd : *i*, as in pol*i*ce : *í*, as in intr*i*gue : *o*, as in c*o*ld : *u*, as in b*u*ll : *ú*, as in s*u*re.

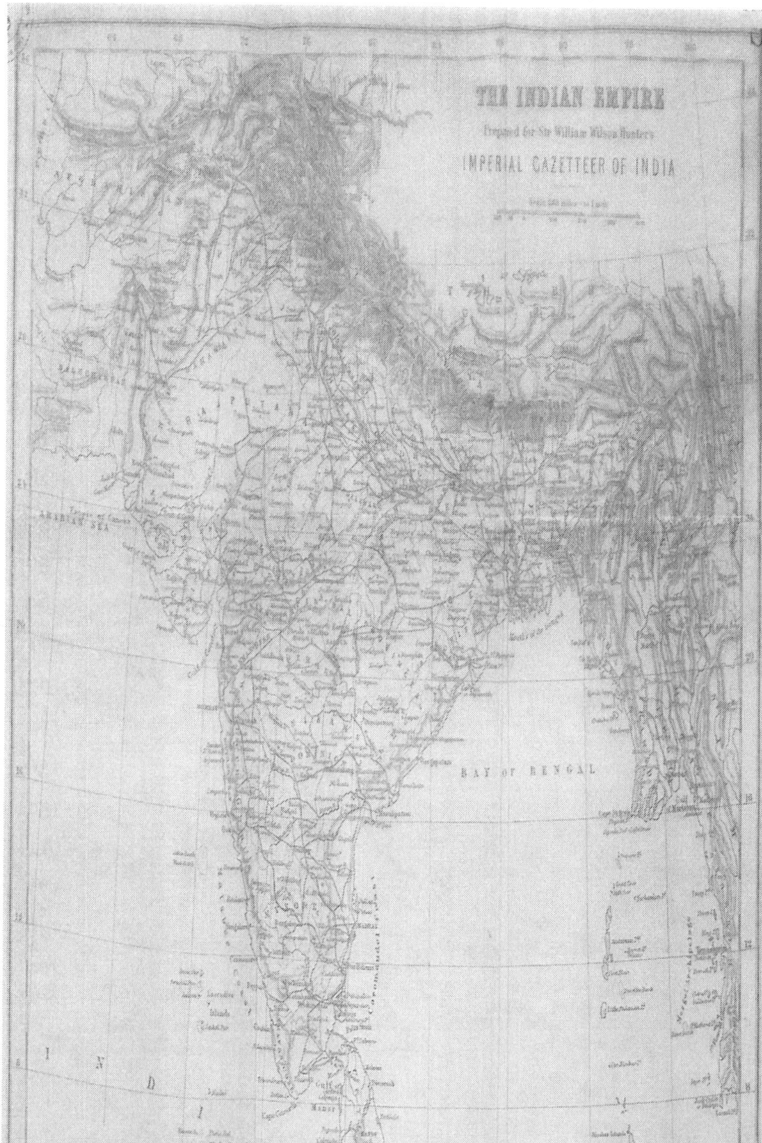

THE INDIAN EMPIRE
Prepared for Sir William Wilson Hunter's
IMPERIAL GAZETTEER OF INDIA
ARABIAN SEA
BAY OF BENGAL
I N D I A N O C E A N
Long. E. of Greenwich

LORD HARDINGE

CHAPTER I

Birth and Boyhood

Henry, first Viscount Hardinge of Lahore and King's Newton, was descended from a family that had been long settled at King's Newton in Derbyshire, where the name can be traced back among the local landowners to the reign of Henry VI. His ancestor at the time of the Great Rebellion was Sir Robert Hardinge, who raised a troop of horse for Charles I, and was knighted after the Restoration. His monument in the parish church of Melbourne (a fine old Norman building) records that he was 'a faithful servant to God, the King, the Church of England, and his country in the worst times.' This monument, together with others in the Hardinge chancel, was restored by the Governor-General before he went to India. King's Newton Hall, built in 1563, was a good example of the Tudor architecture of that period. Unfortunately, it was destroyed by fire in 1859; all that now remains of it is a picturesque ruin, overgrown with ivy and other creepers. The estate had been sold in 1796 to Lord Melbourne, and has now passed into the possession of Lord Cowper.

Lord Hardinge was born at Wrotham, in Kent, on 30th March, 1785. He was the third son of the Rev. Henry Hardinge, rector of Stanhope, in Durham, by his marriage with Frances, daughter of James Best of Park House, Boxley, Kent.

The eldest son, Charles, succeeded to the baronetcy which had been conferred upon his uncle, Sir Richard Hardinge of Lurran, County Fermanagh, with remainder to his heirs general. Sir Charles sold the Irish estate and purchased Bounds Park in Kent. Having taken holy orders, he held the vicarage of Tunbridge from 1809 until his death in 1864.

The second son, George, distinguished himself highly in the Navy, until his career was cut short by an early death. In March, 1808, while cruising off the coast of Ceylon, in command of the 'San Fiorenzo' (36 guns and 186 men), he fell in with the 'Piédmontaise,' a French frigate carrying 50 guns and 566 men. She was boarded and captured, but Captain Hardinge fell mortally wounded at the very moment of victory. He was only in his twenty-seventh year. A monument was erected to his memory in St. Paul's by Parliament, and another of larger dimensions at Bombay, subscribed for by the merchants residing in that Presidency.

The youngest son, Richard, entered the Royal Artillery. Like his brother Henry, he saw service during the Peninsular War and in the Waterloo campaign, and rose to the rank of Major-General.

Mention, too, should be made of his uncle, George Hardinge, well known as a lawyer, scholar, and literary critic. After a successful career at the Bar and in Parliament, he was appointed Judge of the three Welsh counties of Brecon, Glamorgan, and Radnor. His wife was Lucy, daughter of R. Long of Hinxton, Cambridgeshire, whose portrait by Sir Joshua Reynolds is considered one of his finest works[1]. After his death, his *Miscellaneous Writings* were published by his friend James Nichols (3 vols., 1818).

Henry, the future Governor-General, passed his childhood at The Grove, near Sevenoaks, under the charge of two maiden aunts, whom he ever spoke of with great affection. Before entering the army he was for some time at school at Durham; and he used to relate how he was always told off by his school-fellows for climbing the buttresses of the Cathedral and other services of danger in search of birds'-nests. When a boy, he was short in stature; and he would tell how his aunts made him hang with his arms on a door in order to stimulate his growth. The result of this treatment was in their minds satisfactory; for, although never a tall man, he passed

[1] This portrait of Mrs. George Hardinge was for some years lost. When Mr. Tom Taylor made enquiries from the family respecting its whereabouts, no information could be given; but it afterwards turned up in the possession of Lord Clanricarde. The mezzotint engraving of the picture is well known.

muster as to height when he was gazetted to his first regiment, the Queen's Rangers, in 1799, and joined it at the age of fifteen.

The regiment was then stationed in Canada, and there Hardinge remained until it was brought home to England after the Peace of Amiens. One of the anecdotes he often told was how, when he was returning one evening from mess at Montreal, his attention was drawn to a group of three or four men who were assaulting and rifling the pockets of a man on the ground. Drawing his sword, he threatened their lives; and such was the cowardice of these bullies that, seeing an officer in uniform, they fled, after a short resistance. On going up to the injured man he found it was a Mr. Edward Ellice, who was naturally profuse in his thanks. The assailants were captured, and brought up the next morning before the magistrate. The strongest evidence against them was the discovery of young Hardinge's military 'pigtail' in one of their pockets. This incident led to a lasting friendship between Ellice and Hardinge. Both became Cabinet Ministers, and each held the office of Secretary at War. Mr. Ellice was a distinguished member of the Whig party, and the two had often amicable contests on the floor of the House of Commons. On one occasion, on a military committee of which both were members, Sir Henry, irritated at some expressions that had fallen from his old friend, exclaimed, 'Ah! Ellice, I almost begin to think it would have been better if I had not saved your life in the streets of Montreal.'

CHAPTER II

The Peninsular War and Waterloo Campaign

In 1804 Hardinge was promoted to a company in the 57th Foot, and shortly afterwards was entered as a student at the senior department of the Royal Military College, then at High Wycombe, under General Jarry. There he worked with such energy and success that, on leaving the College, he was selected to fill a staff appointment in the Quarter-Master-General's department under Sir Brent Spencer, who commanded the expedition sent out to the Peninsula in 1807.

In 1808 Sir Brent Spencer's force was united with that which had sailed from Ireland under Sir Arthur Wellesley. The result of this campaign was the complete defeat of Junot's *corps d'armée*; and on this and other occasions the lessons which Hardinge had learned at the senior department of the Military College were, as he often mentioned in later life, of the greatest practical benefit. He had the good fortune to be present at the battles of Roliça and Vimiera, in the latter of which he was severely wounded.

Sir Benjamin D'Urban, the Quarter-Master-General of the Portuguese army, in a letter dated from the field (June 22nd, 1808), writes respecting him in the following terms:—'I grieve to tell you that our inestimable friend, Captain Hardinge, was wounded in the hottest point of attack. It is his custom to be foremost in every attack, where an unaffected gallantry of spirit irresistibly carries him. Here he was conspicuous where all were brave, and it is a consolation to know that there is not a man in this army who does not regret this misfortune. The wound is in the bottom of the left side, under the lowest rib. The ball passed through, and the surgeons are of opinion that nothing is injured which can warrant any apprehension of a bad result. At the same time, it would be deceiving you to say that he is not severely wounded, or that a perfect recovery may not be tedious because of the sinews which the ball has passed through. I will not attempt to tell you how I lament this accident. As a friend with whom I have lived above four years in the greatest intimacy, whose society has formed part of my happiness, and whom I hold in the truest affection; as a soldier, whose conduct and courage I have often admired; and as a man whose virtues I esteem and venerate—you who know him may well judge how deeply I feel interested in him. He is now an example of fortitude and tranquillity; and highly as I thought of him before, it remained for me to see him in his present state to be aware of *all* the excellences of his nature.'

And here I am induced to give the following

extracts from a letter which Hardinge himself wrote to his relative, Lord Camden, in August, 1808, giving interesting details of the battle of Vimiera. 'Be assured that I should have written the day after the action on the 21st, had I not been prevented by a numbness in my right hand occasioned by my wound.' The letter then proceeds to describe how our troops, after having forced the heights and pass, beneath which the village of Roliça stands, had frustrated all attempts of the enemy to harass their advance, and how the position of Vimiera was taken up. The army having been reinforced by the troops under Generals Anstruther and Ackland on the morning of the 21st, General Ferguson's brigade was ordered to the left, supported by the brigade under General Nightingale and covered by the skirmishers of the 95th, now the Rifle Brigade. The French began the attack on the centre, and were received with so hot a fire that before they had reached the valley they turned and fled. On the left of the British centre two strong columns of the enemy advanced, the officers and men 'evincing a resolution and steady courage improved by discipline.' Their commander, Colonel Patervil, was shot down in the act of carrying his hat on the point of his sword, the whole mass shouting '*En avant.*'

Let me again quote Hardinge's own words at this juncture:—'H. M.'s 50th and 43rd received them steadily; then, wheeling up four companies, made a noble charge upon four times their number, overthrowing all before them and precluding the power to rally. The carnage was dreadful, and the calculation is that in this one attack they lost 1200 men. The Portuguese horse took this opportunity of making a charge, but galloped away when they were near the enemy, as they have always done. The handful of British performed wonders. Then along the whole line the enemy began to waver. General Farquharson's brigade with General Spencer's charged the line and guns, when they fled in confusion, leaving the whole of the latter in our possession.'

In this letter, too, he gives details of the estimation in which the British force was held by the enemy. 'The courage of British troops in the field admits of no doubt, but it is a source of peculiar satisfaction to have discovered that in skill and manœuvring light troops we are in no way inferior to the French.' As to our artillery, 'they confess ours to be superior to any of theirs. They fired much, and we have scarcely a man wounded by artillery fire. The French cavalry simply disgraced themselves.'

The next extract describes the dispute that took place on the halt of the British force, as soon as the enemy were routed. It is specially interesting, as being the contemporary record of an eye-witness:—'Sir H. Burrard arrived on the field in the midst of the attack on the left. He made no offer to assume the command. When the enemy were in full retreat, Sir A. Wellesley asked for the guides to Torres Vedras. It was replied that they were at hand, and Farquharson's brigade was ordered to advance, when it received positive orders from Sir H. Burrard not to move. Farquharson begged that he might do so on his own responsibility—not one step of concession could this message obtain. Sir A. Wellesley rode up, and asked if it was in orders that the troops should not advance. Angry words then passed, but not a move was made.'

After observing that the British force was comparatively fresh, that the reserves were at hand with an ample supply of stores and ammunition, that meat and biscuits for two days were in every haversack, and that the enemy were in a state of complete demoralisation, Hardinge justly condemns this inactivity. The enemy had lost 3000 men and all their guns; their columns were three miles asunder, while they had to march eight miles to reach Torres Vedras. Hardinge maintains that an advance would in all probability have put the finishing stroke to a glorious victory. He declares that from 1 p.m. on that day the murmurs of the army were loud and deep, that the officers of Sir A. Wellesley's corps were disgusted, and that inefficiency in council was apparent in every day's orders.

The victory at Vimiera led to the Convention of Cintra, concerning which there was much discussion when the news reached England, and which its advocates had no easy task in defending.

At the close of the year 1808 Hardinge was so far recovered from his wound as to be able to carry important despatches to Sir John Moore, performing the journey to Benevente with singular rapidity. We then find him with the rear-guard of Sir John Moore's force during the arduous retreat to Corunna, ending in that brilliant engagement which purchased the safe embarkation of the army at the price of its commander's life. As Hardinge was, I believe, almost the only officer by the side of Sir John Moore when he received his fatal wound, it may be worth while to quote his own description of the scene:—

'The circumstances which deprived the army of its gallant commander, Sir J. Moore, are of too interesting a nature not to be made public for the admiration of his countrymen; but I trust that the instance of fortitude and heroism of which I was a witness may also have another effect—that of affording some consolation to his relatives and friends. I had been ordered by the Commander-in-Chief to desire a battalion of Guards to advance, which battalion was intended to have dislodged a corps of the enemy from a large house and garden on the opposite side of the valley; and I was pointing out to the General the situation of the battalion, when a shot from the enemy's battery carried off his left shoulder and part of the collar bone. The violence of the shock threw him off his horse; but not a muscle of his face altered, nor did a sigh betray the least sensation of pain. The blood flowed fast, but the attempt to stop it with my sash was useless from the size of the wound. Sir John assented to being removed in a blanket to the rear. In raising him for that purpose, his sword hanging on his wounded side became entangled in his legs. In the act of my unbuckling it, he said in his usual tone, "It is as well as it is: I had rather it should go out of the field with me." Observing the resolution and composure of his features, I caught at the hope that I might be mistaken in my fears of the wound being mortal, and remarked that I trusted when the surgeon dressed the wound he would be spared to us and recover. "No, Hardinge," he said, "I feel that to be impossible."'

This letter appears in *Moore's Campaign in Spain*, which was published by his brother, Mr. J. C. Moore, in 1809.

Returning to England the same year, Hardinge was promoted to a majority, and went back at once to Portugal on the staff of Sir W. Beresford, who had been entrusted with the organization of the Portuguese army. As Deputy-Quarter-Master-General he was present at the passage of the Douro and other actions. Still attached to Beresford's staff, he served with the army of observation in Castile, and was thanked in General Orders issued at Guizo, May, 1809. The next campaign was the famous defensive one of 1810, when Wellington out-manœuvred Masséna with conspicuous success. After the battle of Busaco, Hardinge was mentioned in Sir W. Beresford's despatch to the Portuguese Regency. In the operations of the year 1811 he was again actively employed, and the part he took in the siege of Badajos and the storming of the Fort of Picarina was mentioned in the official despatches.

But it was on the hard-fought field of Albuera that Hardinge's reputation was established as a staff-officer of no ordinary distinction. Sir W. Napier, who has painted in vivid language the heroic struggles which took place on the plateau above the Albuera river, thus describes the turning-point of the engagement:—'Whilst the Marshal was thus preparing to resign the contest, Captain Hardinge[1] boldly ordered General Cole to advance with the Fourth Division. Then, riding to Abercrombie's brigade, he directed him to push forward into the fight. The die being cast, Beresford acquiesced, and the terrible battle was continued. Cole led the Fusiliers up the contested height, when for a moment Houghton's brigade could no longer hold its ground. The Fusiliers soon mounted the hill, and appeared on the right of Houghton's brigade simultaneously with the advance of Abercrombie on the left. Such a line issuing from the smoke startled the enemy's masses. The Fusilier Battalion reeled and wavered. It was then seen with what a majesty the British soldier fights. Suddenly recovering, they closed on their terrible enemies. Then the French reserves endeavoured to maintain the fight. The rain flowed in torrents, discoloured with blood, and 1500 men out of 6000 unconquerable British soldiers stood triumphant on that fated hill.'

In 1829 strictures were published on Napier's ac-

[1] He was then only twenty-five years of age.

count of the battle by an anonymous military critic. In the extract above quoted, Napier had implied that at one moment thoughts of retreat had crossed Beresford's mind. This Hardinge always denied. In his MS. notes on the battle, written in 1830, he maintains that no order to retire was ever given, nor was there any evidence to show that any one had carried or meditated such an order.

In his further strictures, the anonymous critic gives his version of the advance of the Fourth Division under Cole:—'Captain Hardinge having given his message to General Lumley, proceeded to Sir Lowry Cole's position. What the motives were which influenced him at that moment after the lapse of so many years *he may not be able himself to assign*; but having been with Sir W. Beresford when he attempted to attack the enemy's left with the Spaniards, and, seeing General Cole's position on the reverse of the ridge and that Hamilton was not there, it is probable that these circumstances had their influence and induced him *to propose* to Cole to advance his Division and charge the enemy. That excellent officer, not having any orders, was with difficulty persuaded to adopt the course which had been suggested. As Cole came into contact with the French, the other parts of the line charged simultaneously; and victory from that moment was gained.'

Now read Hardinge's own account of the affair, taken from MS. notes written in 1830. In reply to the suggestion that he probably would not be able to explain his motives for this action, he simply replies that 'the only motive in moving the Division was to attack the enemy and defeat that enemy. I would add this to the reasons subsequently given, *that I thought the battle desperate, and that nothing but an offensive flank movement could retrieve it.*' With regard to the decisive movement of the day, he states :—'The instant Cole's Division was in movement, and his left brigade approached the right of Houghton, I went to Abercrombie's brigade and authorized him to deploy and move past Houghton's left. While Houghton's brigade held the hill, Myers and Abercrombie passed the flanks on the right and left, and made a simultaneous attack on the enemy, who began to waver and then went off to the rear. Myers and Abercrombie, in my opinion, decided the fate of the day.'

Sir B. D'Urban, the Quarter-Master-General of the Portuguese army, published in the same year an account of the battle of Albuera, in which he maintains that Colonel Hardinge had simply anticipated Beresford's order. But there is no evidence that any such order was contemplated by Beresford, who, in his official account of the battle, merely records the fact that Cole's Division advanced at this particular crisis.

I have inserted the above extracts from Hardinge's MS. notes, because they show that he alone was responsible for Cole's advance, and that Napier was justified in attributing to him the credit of being the sole originator of the movement. I believe I am correct in stating that the advance of these brigades, and that alone, turned the tide of this memorable action. Lord Hardinge's equestrian statue by Foley, R.A., on the Maidan at Calcutta, records on its pedestal the part he took in this great victory—a victory which was all-important in its results on the subsequent operations in the Peninsula.

For his services at Albuera, Hardinge received the Portuguese decoration of the Tower and Sword, and was marked out to take a leading part in the remaining operations of the campaign.

Being again wounded severely at Vittoria, he was for a short time placed *hors de combat*; but with his wound still open, causing him great pain, he was determined to go to the front, and was in time to take part in the memorable actions of Salamanca, the Pyrenees, Nive, and Nivelle. He was also present at the siege of St. Sebastian and the operations on the Bidassoa. For these he received the gold medal of distinction, which in those days was the only decoration granted by the Sovereign for services in the field. In the campaign of 1814 he was in command of a Portuguese brigade at Orthez and Toulouse. He was publicly thanked in General Orders and received his tenth decoration. During the whole of the Peninsular War Hardinge was never absent from his duties, except when incapacitated by the severity of his wounds. At the close of the campaign he was promoted to a Lieutenant Colonelcy in the Foot Guards, and was knighted, receiving the K.C.B. when the Order of the Bath was remodelled in January, 1815.

Hardinge accompanied Sir C. Stewart to the Congress of Vienna; and when the war again broke out on Napoleon's return from Elba, he was at once selected as a military and diplomatic officer on Blücher's staff, with the rank of Brigadier-General. Müffling held the corresponding post of Prussian representative at Wellington's head-quarters. Their chief duties were to act as channels of communication between the allied commanders. The Duke had here rightly estimated his officer, such duties requiring not only firmness and military knowledge but consummate tact and judgment.

On June 16th, in the early morning before the memorable battle of Ligny, the Duke of Wellington, being doubtful as to Napoleon's real intentions and considering the small French force in front of Quatre Bras to be only a feint, rode forward to the windmill of Bussy, near Brye, overlooking the position at Ligny, for the purpose of conferring with Blücher on the best plan for uniting against their common enemy. At this moment Sir H. Hardinge, who was engaged in reconnoitring the French position, saw a group of horsemen whom he at first took to be a party of the enemy. On coming nearer he observed that their horses' tails were 'docked,' and at once concluded they were English. Galloping up to the group, and trusting to the speed of his horse in the event of his being mistaken, he came upon the Duke and his staff. Then occurred a conversation, published in *Stanhope's Recollections*, which relates how the Duke expressed his strong disapprobation of the ground taken up by the Prussian army and their disposition. Sir Henry replied that he had already expressed the same misgivings to Marshal Blücher, upon which the Duke remarked, 'Everybody knows their own army best, but if I were to fight with my army here I should expect to be beaten.' A long conversation then took place between Wellington and the three Prussian generals, Blücher, Müffling, and Gneisenau, as to the mode in which the English should be brought up, after which the Duke rode off, promising to come to Blücher's support if he were not himself attacked.

Sir H. Hardinge was present during the whole of the battle of Ligny in attendance on Marshal Blücher, and it was at his suggestion that several movements were made which retarded the success of the French. Towards the close of the day his left-hand was shattered by a round-shot; but with the courage for which he was so distinguished, he had a 'tourniquet' placed on his arm and remained at Blücher's side till the end of the action.

The Marshal's unaffected grief was the best proof of the opinion he entertained of the young officer's military capacity. Being taken to the nearest hut or stable, it was not till midnight that Sir Henry was visited by a Prussian surgeon, who amputated the hand. The operation was not skilfully performed—the ligatures subsequently gave way, and he suffered much from loss of blood. He then sent his brother, Colonel R. Hardinge, R.A., to report the result of the action to the Duke. Colonel R. Hardinge's report was to the effect that the Prussians were beaten but not broken, and ready to fight again. He returned, bringing with him a surgeon of the Life Guards at the Duke's special desire, and a second operation was performed. When the Prussians retired to Wavre, Sir Henry was conveyed at some risk to the Marshal's head-quarters in that town.

It is difficult, after the lapse of many years, to ascertain with accuracy the dates of certain conversations which took place; but Lord Stanhope, an historian of singular accuracy, who probably took the words down in his *Journal* whilst they were fresh in his mind, relates how Sir Henry described the above occurrence. The following is the account given by Lord Stanhope of what took place at Walmer Castle in October, 1837:—'The Duke remarked that at Ligny it was a most extraordinary circumstance that the French did not maintain the position they had won; that the first thing he did on the 17th was to send William Gordon and two squadrons with orders to make their way through all obstacles and let him know what had become of the Prussians; that he came back early on the 17th, having found the French gone off the field of battle and not in possession of Sombreffe. "Yes," said Hardinge, "Blücher had gone back as far as Wavre. I passed that night with my amputated arm lying on some straw in the ante-room. Next morning Blücher sent for me, calling me 'Lieber Freund,' and embracing me. I perceived he smelt strongly of gin and rhubarb. He said to me, 'Ich stinke etwas;' that he had been obliged to take medicine, having been twice ridden over by the cavalry; but he should be quite satisfied if, in conjunction with the Duke, he was able now to defeat his old enemy. I was told there had been a great discussion that night in his rooms, and that Blücher and Grollenau had carried the day for remaining in communication with the English army, but that Gneisenau had great doubts whether they ought not to have fallen back on Liége."'

It has been said that the Marshal, who, as Müffling puts it, was not famous for his strategy, relied implicitly on the military ability of Gneisenau as Chief of the Staff. However, in this case Blücher and Grollenau appear to have fought it out with Gneisenau and carried the day. The above discussions have been so ably commented upon by Colonel Maurice, R.A., in his article in the *United Service Magazine* for July, 1890, that those specially interested in this question need only be referred to it.

As on previous occasions, Sir H. Hardinge did not permit his wound to detain him long from his duty, although from some attendant circumstances he suffered severely from it. He was, of course, unable to accompany the Prussian army to Waterloo, but within a fortnight he had so far recovered as to be conveyed to Paris in an ambulance waggon. He used to relate how he suffered on this journey in his debilitated state, and how on arriving at the barrière at Paris he was met by one of Blücher's staff, who directed him to drive at once to St. Cloud. There an unexpected sight met him. The Palace had been lit up in his honour. Guards holding torches were on the main staircase, and at the top stood Blücher and his staff. He came down the stairs to the ambulance and embraced him, saying, 'Mein lieber Freund, to-night you shall be in comfort; you shall sleep in Marie Louise's bed.' The Guards then carried him up and placed him in the Imperial bed, whilst the staff saluted him with those 'hochs,' for which the Germans are famous. In the morning he espied his servant cleaning his boots in an Imperial jar of Sèvres china. Such are the vicissitudes of war, and the events of 1870 show but too clearly how history repeats itself.

After Waterloo, the Duke of Wellington devoted a special Gazette to Sir H. Hardinge's services, and at a review of the Prussian army on the plains of Sedan in 1816 he took from his own side Napoleon's sword and presented it to him. At the same time the King of Prussia decorated him with the Order of Merit and conferred on him the Red Eagle. Many years afterwards he wore Napoleon's sword in the battles of the Sutlej; and when matters appeared desperate during the eventful night of the 21st December, 1845, he sent his surgeon with it to a place of safety, lest it should fall into the hands of the Sikhs.

During the Peninsular and Waterloo campaigns Sir Henry Hardinge was four times wounded and had four horses shot under him.

CHAPTER III

PARLIAMENTARY LIFE IN ENGLAND

ON the withdrawal of the Army of Occupation, Sir Henry Hardinge was employed in a less stirring field of action. After serving for a short time in the Grenadier Guards, he entered Parliament, and retained a seat there for more than twenty years. He was first returned as member for the city of Durham in the Tory interest at the General Election of 1820, his colleague being Michael Angelo Taylor, the well-known Whig. He was four times re-elected for that constituency without ever encountering any serious opposition. On the dissolution of Parliament occasioned by the demise of the Crown in 1830, he was proposed as a candidate for the county of Northumberland; but both he and his Tory colleague withdrew before the poll. A seat, however, was at once found for him at St. Germans, in Cornwall, which he held for only a few months, vacating it in December of the same year in favour of the poet, Winthrop Mackworth Praed, and being himself returned instead for Newport in the same county. On the disfranchisement of that borough by the Reform Bill of 1832, he was elected for the adjoining borough of Launceston, which was allowed to retain one of its members and where he succeeded a distinguished Anglo-Indian officer, Sir John Malcolm. In spite of a sharp contest on his first election, he continued to sit for Launceston until his appointment to the Governor-Generalship in 1844.

Here should be recorded the happiest event of his life —his marriage in 1821 with Emily, daughter of the first Marquess of Londonderry and sister of Lord Castlereagh. She had previously been married to Mr. J. James, British Minister to the Netherlands and father of the present Lord Northbourne. Those only who knew the virtues of her character and her devotion to her husband in all the trials and changes of mortal life can form a true conception of the happiness of this union. Her last act of devotion was an attempt to join him in India. When sailing from Nice, in 1844, her strength proved unequal to the undertaking, and on the peremptory advice of the doctor she was obliged to retrace her steps. This may be considered as having been providentially ordained—for the consequences of an enervating climate on a frame far from strong might have led to results which her husband shrank from contemplating.

While M.P. for Durham, Sir Henry Hardinge was appointed Clerk of the Ordnance, which office he held from 1823 to 1827. In 1828 he entered the Cabinet as Secretary at War, in succession to Lord Palmerston. For a few months in 1830, and again during the brief Tory Administration of 1834–35, he undertook the yet more responsible duties of Chief Secretary for Ireland.

In 1841, when Peel came back to power with a substantial majority, Sir Henry Hardinge returned to his former office of Secretary at War, which he continued to hold until he was selected to succeed Lord Ellenborough as Governor-General of India.

His political career commenced in troublous times. He witnessed the great struggles which ended in Roman Catholic Emancipation and the passing of the Reform Bill. As Chief Secretary for Ireland, he had to combat the determined attacks of Mr. O'Connell in the House of Commons, and his agitation for the Repeal of the Union. His speeches in Parliament were clear and businesslike; and many were the congratulations from both sides of the House, when he returned from India to take his seat in the House of Lords. He frequently mentioned that, during his tenure of the office of Secretary for Ireland, he had some misgivings as to whether he could successfully encounter the phalanx of Irish orators and able lawyers opposed to him, who, then as now, made the Chief Secretary the object of their incessant hostility. However, he firmly stood the fire of their guns; and when some one, on his Irish appointment being announced, expressed a doubt to the Duke of Wellington as to whether he was a strong enough man for the post, the Duke replied, 'Hardinge will do; he always understands what he undertakes, and undertakes nothing but what he understands.'

In 1834 it fell to his lot to introduce in the House of Commons the Ministerial plan for the settlement of the Irish Tithe question. By this scheme it was proposed that tithes should in future be recoverable only from the landlords; that the tithe-owners should receive only three-quarters of the total amount to which they had been previously entitled; that the tithe should be redeemable by the landlord at twenty years' purchase, calculated upon this diminished rate; that the proceeds thus arising should be invested in land or otherwise for the benefit of the tithe-owners; that the arrears of 1834 should be paid out of the residue of the million advanced from the Consolidated Fund for the benefit of the clergy; and that the advances already made under the 'Million Act' should be remitted. Lord John Russell contended that the bill was identical with that brought in by Mr. Littleton in the preceding session, which had been thrown out by the House of Lords, while Mr. O'Connell condemned the bill *in toto*. But the Ministerial proposal was carried by 213 votes to 198, and a settlement of the question was subsequently effected on these principles.

The following extract from notes of a speech delivered by Sir H. Hardinge in the same year on the Municipal Corporations Act is not without application at the present time:—'Do not let the House be led away by what the hon. and learned member for Dublin [O'Connell] calls justice for Ireland. At one moment he pretends that identity of municipal institutions is justice to Ireland; at another time he makes a crusade through England, inviting the people to join him in an alteration of the House of Lords. This fails; and after abusing the Radicals of England, he falls back upon a total abolition of the tithe and the establishment of the voluntary principle. Now, Her Majesty's Government are opposed to all these "justice" nostrums of the learned member, with the exception of the Bill before the House; and that Bill, if passed into law, will not satisfy him. It is, as he terms it, merely an instalment and a fulcrum on which he is to erect his lever to extort the remainder of his demands. Now, looking to these demands, which are supported by gentlemen opposite in terms of equal justice to Ireland, let me ask any calm and moderate statesman whether the Irish people are really insulted because there is a refusal to pass laws of the same nature and principle as those passed for England. The real principle, for all practical purposes, appears to be to consider the social, political and religious state of the country, and to legislate in such a manner as to afford equal protection to every profession and party, and to give equal enjoyment of all rights and privileges to every subject.'

Many fundamental changes have since taken place in Ireland. The Church has been disestablished and disendowed. The tenure of land has been radically altered. The franchise has been fixed on a democratic basis. And yet the cry is still heard for further and more sweeping reforms; the struggle is as keen as ever.

As Secretary at War, Sir Henry Hardinge was

enabled to confer lasting benefits on the rank and file of the army, by which he earned the title of the 'Soldier's Friend.' His authority as a statesman and a military man of long official experience was quoted as recently as last year (1890) during the enquiry of Lord Hartington's Commission on Army and Navy Organisation. In paragraph 79 of that Report it is stated that the principle that the Commander-in-Chief could claim no authority in matters of finance was strongly upheld by Lord Hardinge in 1837. He held that the exclusive control over public money voted for military purposes rested with the Secretary at War. It was also maintained by the Duke of Wellington, who asserted before the Finance Committee in 1828 that the Commander-in-Chief has no power of giving an allowance to anybody or of incurring any expense whatever. Again, in paragraph 80 of the same Report, it is mentioned that further powers were claimed for the Secretary at War by Lord Hardinge, who stated in 1832, 'I think that the Secretary at War is, in a constitutional point of view, the proper person to draw up the Mutiny Bill and Articles of War. He is bound to stand between the civil subject and the military; and it is his duty to take care that the civil part of the community are properly protected, and that those who enter the army are not treated in an unnecessarily strict manner. I must maintain that it is, in a constitutional point of view, the duty of a Secretary at War to be responsible for all military transactions to this House and the country.'

These are weighty opinions, coming from one who had no small experience of the working of the military departments. They were always held by his predecessor, the Duke of Wellington, as well as by H.R.H. the present Commander-in-Chief.

On the subject of recruiting for the army Sir Henry Hardinge was opposed, as most military men are, to the enlistment of soldiers under nineteen years of age. In a Memorandum on recruiting, written in 1829, he recorded that the 7th Foot in the Peninsula lost in one year 246 men by disease, of whom 169 were recruits recently landed; whilst out of 1145 old soldiers only 77 died. Similarly, in the 40th Foot in the same campaign, out of 170 recruits 104 were lost to the service from the same causes. He always insisted on the supreme importance of not sending men under twenty years of age upon foreign service. These opinions he still held when he was Commander-in-Chief during the Crimean War; but such was the pressure then placed on the resources of the country from the duration of the siege of Sebastopol and other causes, that the Government was obliged to reinforce Lord Raglan's army in the trenches with young recruits, who perished in large numbers as rapidly as in the Peninsula. Even now, in a time of profound peace, drafts are sometimes sent to India containing a considerable proportion of boys under twenty, a state of things which is one of the great difficulties of maintaining an Indian army by a system of short service.

During his parliamentary career as Secretary at

War, Sir Henry Hardinge was constantly confronted by Mr. Joseph Hume, the well-known Radical M.P. for Montrose, who examined and criticised the estimates for the army with special ability. In the year 1853, when a parliamentary committee was enquiring into the renewal of the East India Company's Charter, Mr. Hume cross-questioned him upon his distribution of patronage in India. Lord Hardinge, amongst other appointments referred to, replied that one of the best men he had brought to the front was a man of extreme democratic views. 'Ah!' said Joseph Hume, 'then you found out that an out-and-out Radical was not such a bad fellow after all[1].'

To Sir H. Hardinge is due also the humane prohibition against firing on mobs by the military. The instructions are now much more precise as to the circumstances under which the soldier is to supersede the magistrate. He was an advocate of corporal punishment in the army, as necessary for the preservation of discipline, whenever its abolition was proposed in Parliament. Of this he was so conscientiously convinced that one of the acts which marked his Indian administration was the restoration of flogging in the Native army, which had been abolished by Lord William Bentinck. This was looked upon as a very hazardous undertaking, but the result was so far satisfactory that corporal

[1] Being a member of that Committee, I heard Mr. Hume use these words.

punishment at once became practically a dead letter in the Native army.

The following Memorandum, drawn up in 1826, when Sir H. Hardinge was Clerk of the Ordnance is interesting, as showing the views he advocated with regard to the want of preparation and organisation which he thought existed at that period:—'The expediency,' he remarks, 'of being prepared at all times for a renewal of war, as it regards the security of the country and its colonies, and the power of making early and vigorous offensive exertions, cannot admit of a doubt. This object, it is conceived, may be assisted by carefully looking into every branch of the Ordnance establishment as it now is [in 1826] after ten years of peace. Assuming the establishment to rest on its present basis, and that all augmentations in case of war have to be provided for, it will be desirable to ascertain whether the Department, in all its parts dispersed over this vast empire, is in that state of order and readiness in which it ought to be to meet a sudden renewal of hostilities, to discover those parts which are defective, to apply remedies, to distribute the Ordnance resources in just proportions to its necessary wants, so that by previous arrangement every measure of a general and local nature should be decided in order to avoid delay at the moment of action, and that the means and mode of augmenting each branch with rapidity should be calculated and fixed beforehand, thereby accomplishing the double purpose of putting everything in a secure state of defence, and in a fit state for rapid augmentation.'

The Memorandum states that this question must become more pressing the longer we remain at peace. 'As the feeling and recollection of the late war subsides, the more confirmed becomes the habit of looking at all our establishments as a sort of arrangement limited to the duties required of them in peace, without reference to a state of preparation for war.' It is further maintained in the same Memorandum that 'we ought to redouble our efforts to counteract the ill effects of over-reduction for all the various parts of which the military force of the empire is composed. The Ordnance establishments, from the scientific nature of their details, are those which are the slowest to bring to perfection. The clamour raised against many of these establishments is followed by the assertion that the manufacturing departments should be put down, and that the private mills and manufacturing agencies of Birmingham should supply our wants, without such establishments as Enfield, Waltham, &c.'

Sir H. Hardinge also observes that 'on the breaking out of the Revolutionary War the inefficiency of the army did not proceed so much from any inferiority of discipline, as from the total break-down of its establishments. The troops constantly distinguished themselves, but the artillery department was so unwieldy that the guns were an impediment instead of affording assistance to the troops. The army had no field-train, no waggon-train, and can hardly be said to have had a Commissariat or a Medical Department. The steady successes at the end of the war show that, under proper direction, the country can and ought to rely on its national troops, and that the army can never be effective unless its military establishments are kept in efficiency in time of peace, of which the most important are under the direction of the Ordnance Department.' He then concludes by saying that 'the most important question to be thoroughly looked into is the question of coast-defence—how the batteries should be armed, where placed, and how the additional expense should be met, especially as regards Ireland, where, from the temper of the people, a proper amount of force should be always distributed.'

The principles thus advocated in 1826 have not lost their importance at the present day. Royal Commissions and Departmental Committees without number have enquired year after year into all these questions; but nothing has been practically done until recently, when estimates have been passed providing for our coast-defences at home and abroad. Guns, however, like ships, are ever changing as to type. Augmentations in numbers are sanctioned only to be cut down again in a succeeding session, and with the view of squaring a popular budget, while departments are remodelled for the purpose of centralizing or dispersing the responsibility of the different heads. He would be a bold man, whether statesman or soldier, who would maintain that everything has even now been finally settled on a secure basis.

In 1829, as Secretary at War, Sir Henry Hardinge revised and consolidated the system of pensions which had existed since 1806. The necessity for this revision arose from the fact that the number of pensioners of fourteen years' service and upwards had increased since 1817 from 64,000 to 84,000, and including the artillery to 94,000; while the number of admissions to the list exceeded the number of deaths by 500 annually. Under the existing system, 1715 men had been pensioned off at the average age of twenty-four years, most of whom had completed only four or five years' service. That short-service soldiers should be pensioned for life at so early an age was attributable in a great measure to a statute of George III, under which soldiers' pensions, formerly dependent upon royal bounty, became vested interests under the guarantee of an Act of Parliament. Moreover, pensions were often granted to men discharged for every sort of military crime, contrary no doubt to what were the intentions of Parliament.

All this could only be corrected, according to the views of Sir H. Hardinge, by cancelling all previous warrants and substituting a fresh system. Under the new warrant, soldiers of only fourteen years' service were allowed a temporary and conditional pension; while long and faithful service was duly recognised. It was, at the same time, not retrospective. The pension for wounds remained the same as had been laid down in 1812; but the rate for length of service was increased from 1s. to 1s. 2d. *per diem* after certain periods. Soldiers of fourteen years' service received in future only a gratuity in proportion to their length of service. This substitution of gratuity instead of pension for short service put a stop to the practice of 'malingering,' which the previous system had encouraged by giving a pension to every man discharged on the ground of disability.

In a discussion with Sir Herbert Taylor, Sir H. Hardinge's own words are these:—'I state twenty-one years to be a fair term of service; efficiency is true economy, and is the great principle by which the army should be regulated.' I quote these passages to show that the decrease of the charge for pensions was not the chief object of the warrant, but that efficiency, justice to the old soldier, and the substitution of the principle of pensions for long service instead of for disability, formed the basis on which it was to be worked. Lord Hill, Lord Beresford, Sir George Murray, and many others of great military experience concurred, as well as the Duke of Wellington, who said:—'I contend that disability on account of disease is not merit—it may more properly be termed demerit.' These were the main features of the warrant of 1829, and they met with general approval. Modifications have been subsequently introduced, but the principles applied to long service by Sir H. Hardinge still remain in force.

The short service of seven years has since been established; but all non-commissioned officers, as well as rank and file, can re-engage, if approved of by their commanding officer, and on certain other conditions, with the object of earning the pension after completing twenty-one years' total service. Short service has, no doubt, provided the army with a valuable reserve. But it has, like every other scheme, its shortcomings and drawbacks. The problem which still remains to be solved is whether our recruiting powers will at all times be found equal to the emergency, combined with the drain upon the finances of India caused by bringing home the time-expired men.

In dealing with the political career of Sir H. Hardinge, the prominent part he took in the debates on the Carlist War in 1836 and 1837 must not be passed over. On the death of King Ferdinand, the Ministers of England and France saw the necessity of maintaining the title of Isabella to the throne of Spain; she became bound to us as we became bound to her and the other Powers by the Quadruple Treaty, which was signed in 1834. The object of this Treaty, as stated in its principal articles, was the establishment of peace by the expulsion of the Infantas from Portugal, where Don Carlos and his adherents were not only supporting Don Miguel, but entering into every sort of intrigue to subvert the Spanish Monarchy. By the third article, England engaged to co-operate with a naval force in the operations to be undertaken by the troops of Spain and Portugal. Shortly after the signing of the Treaty, Lord Palmerston had issued an Order in Council suspending the Foreign Enlistment

Act in favour of Queen Isabella. Colonel (afterwards Sir) De Lacy Evans was appointed to command the Auxiliary Legion, and landed at St. Sebastian in July, 1835. The Tory party in Parliament vigorously assailed this policy. It was contended on their part that the Government had gone beyond—and had even contravened—the terms of the Treaty. In 1837 a motion was brought forward condemning the Order in Council. Mr. Roebuck supported it, with the view of putting an end to the policy of intervention in the affairs of the Continent, while Lord Palmerston replied in his happiest vein. The House divided, and the motion was negatived by a majority of thirty-six votes.

In the meantime, Sir De Lacy Evans's Legion had been employed in raising the siege of Bilbao, in conjunction with the naval force under Lord John Hay. Other operations followed, in which the Legion fought gallantly, but under the disadvantages of want of training, want of supplies, and want of officers of experience. This led to the return of Sir De Lacy Evans to England, where he had to defend himself against the numerous critics who had sprung up. It was on this occasion that Sir H. Hardinge made one of his forcible speeches, in reply to the explanations offered by the commander of the Legion in the House of Commons. He reminded Sir De Lacy that the Liberal and Tory press had criticised him with equal asperity. He compared the medical arrangements made by the Spanish Government with those of the Peninsular War, showing that the loss by sickness in the Duke of Wellington's army was one in thirty, whilst the Legion lost one in five from the same causes—sixty officers and 2000 men had died in one winter from disease, misery, and starvation, without pay and without rations. He denounced the conduct of the Spanish Government as infamous. He next found fault with Sir De Lacy Evans for having issued an order on his arrival at St. Sebastian that a soldier for certain offences should receive two dozen lashes without a court-martial, he himself having voted steadily in Parliament for the abolition of corporal punishment.

After denouncing Don Carlos's Darango Decree, he alluded to the retreat from Ernani: 'When the gallant officer [Sir De L. Evans] spoke of the retreat at Ernani as a "mischance," his force of 14,000 men having lost four hundred men in the retreat, the efforts of the Legion cannot have been very great.' When he criticised their conduct on that occasion, his criticisms were only equalled by those of the gallant officer himself in his own despatch; after such a despatch he considered the mischief irremediable, and that the Legion could do no more good. This defeat, he held, was owing to the 'insubordination which had arisen from the gross neglect of the Spanish Government.' He then showed that want of communication with Espartero and the other generals had created a disaster; and a disaster on the field of battle was much worse, and a very different thing from a retreat, which (as at Corunna) might be a brilliant achievement. He further stated that the Duke of Wellington's Peninsular army had never attacked a position which they did not take, or defended a position which they did not keep. He remarked that this reminded him of an anecdote told of Napoleon by General Foy: Napoleon was observing that the British force was defending a position in which it had been vigorously attacked. 'Yes,' said General Foy, 'these English always keep a position when they get it.' Napoleon said it was always so. He knew of no instance to the contrary. 'Yes,' said Foy, 'the contrary occurred at the battle of Almanza.' 'But at that battle,' said Napoleon, 'the French army was commanded by the Duke of Berwick, an Englishman, and the English by Ruvigny Lord Galway, a Frenchman.'

The *Times*, in reviewing the debate, remarked that Sir De L. Evans was specially unfortunate in being answered by Sir H. Hardinge, whose comments were unanswerable, and who retracted nothing.

Sir Henry Hardinge's political views were essentially Conservative. He lived at a time when the excitement of party politics ran high, and when a sharp line of demarcation divided the contending factions in Parliament. A political opponent has described him as a warm but generous adversary, liable to be roused by the slightest imputation, but one who never allowed the sun to go down upon his wrath. When, on his return from India, a dinner in his honour was given at the Carlton Club by the Conservative party, he remarked, in reply to the

Chairman's speech, that he went to India a Conservative, and that his opinions had undergone no change.

When affairs of honour, as they were termed in those days, were in vogue, Sir Henry Hardinge was frequently appealed to for advice by the most eminent men in public life. No man possessed a greater reputation for sound judgment and tact in matters requiring the most delicate handling, and both the Duke of Wellington and Sir Robert Peel had the advantage of his advice on several occasions. The most memorable of these was the meeting which took place between the Duke of Wellington and Lord Winchelsea in 1829.

During his political career it was to Peel that Sir Henry Hardinge was most devotedly attached. The following letter shows the affectionate terms on which they corresponded. It was written in reply to a private account of the battle of Firozsháh, which the Governor-General had sent home to him.

'1846.

'MY DEAR HARDINGE,

'Your loss has been very severe. It demonstrates the extent of danger and the necessity for unparalleled exertion. We are astonished at the numbers, the power of concentration, and the skill and courage of the enemy. On all matters of reinforcement, I hope Lord Ripon will write to you as fully as the short time will allow. We shall lay some of your letters on the table of the House, tending to show the policy which you had resolved to pursue, and the unprovoked and wicked aggression which you have repelled. Your escape and that of your sons, amid all the perils that surrounded you, has filled us with delight. Lady Peel is greatly pleased that you thought of her amid the pressure of such events as those in the midst of which your letter was written.

'My boy (William)[1] is just come home from the Sandwich Islands, being sent home after a personal survey of the Oregon, with despatches.

'I think we shall be able to preserve peace with the United States, notwithstanding the blustering of Polk and the American Congress.

'God bless you, my dear Hardinge. Excuse my hurried letter. I am fighting a desperate battle here. Shall probably drive my opponents across the Sutlej, but what is to come afterwards, I know not.

'Ever affectionately yours,

'R. PEEL.'

The above letter is now preserved in a case at the National Portrait Gallery, with others written by the most eminent men of the day.

I may here mention another letter, addressed by Sir Robert Peel to Sir Henry Hardinge, on the eve of his departure for India. Peel mentions how he had noticed that Hardinge wore only the ribbon of a

[1] Sir William Peel, R.N., afterwards so highly distinguished in the Crimea and in the Mutiny.

Prussian Order, that his military services were well known, and that he proposed to confer on him the Grand Cross of the Bath in the civil division, in recognition of the political services he had rendered to the country.

In 1842 peace had been made with China, and the Kábul disaster was avenged by the entry of Pollock's army into the Afghán capital, while Peel's Cabinet bade fair to enjoy public confidence till the Irish famine broke up the hitherto united party, led by such distinguished statesmen as Lord Aberdeen, Mr. Sidney Herbert, Mr. Stanley (Lord Derby), Mr. Gladstone, and Sir J. Graham. With all these Sir H. Hardinge was on terms of the closest confidence and intimacy. All of them have left the scene of their labours, with one brilliant exception, whose name must occur to every one in the political world.

It would not be within the scope of this Memoir to review the conduct of Lord Ellenborough as Governor-General of India (1842–44) and his recall. He was the kinsman by marriage of Sir H. Hardinge, and corresponded with him during his Indian administration. When he left India, he prided himself on the state of profound peace in which he had left the country. Whether that peace could be preserved was a matter which gave rise to much speculation; and without doubt the selection of a distinguished soldier, who also possessed the experience of a Cabinet Minister, rather pointed to the anticipation of war. A few years before, on the receipt of the news of the Kábul disasters (1842), Sir Henry Hardinge had been pressed to accept the command of the Indian army, which for urgent private reasons he was compelled to decline. Now, on being offered the higher office of Governor-General, he felt it an imperative duty to waive all personal considerations. This is so well expressed in a speech of Sir R. Peel's, on moving a vote of thanks in Parliament, on April 2nd, 1846, to the Army of the Sutlej, that I feel the following extract should be reproduced: 'He made a great sacrifice, from a sense of public duty. My gallant friend held a prominent place in the councils of Her Majesty; he was, without reference to party divisions, held in great esteem in this House, as well by his political opponents as by his political friends. He was regarded by the army of this country as its friend, because he was the friend of justice to all ranks. It was proposed to him—at a time of life when perhaps ambition is a less powerful stimulus than it might have been at an earlier period—it was proposed to him to relinquish his place in the councils of the Sovereign, and to forego the satisfaction he must have felt at what he could not fail to see, that he was an object of general respect and esteem.' Such words are no ordinary tribute to his memory, especially when uttered by so great a statesman.

Read, too, the parting words of the Chairman (Captain Shepherd) of the Court of Directors, addressed to Sir H. Hardinge at a farewell banquet of the Court, June, 1844: 'By our latest intelligence we are induced to hope that peace will be preserved in India. I need not say that it is our anxious wish that it should be so. You, sir, know how great are the evils of war. And we feel confident that, while ever ready to maintain unimpaired the honour of the country and the supremacy of our arms, your policy will be essentially pacific. It has always been the desire of the Court that the government of the East India Company should be eminently just, moderate, and conciliatory; but the supremacy of our power must be maintained when necessary by the force of our arms.' May it not be said that Sir H. Hardinge's subsequent policy carried out almost to the letter the above instructions?

In the preceding pages the early life and political career of Sir H. Hardinge have been briefly sketched, the limits of this Memoir not admitting of further detail. Few soldiers of the present century can point to such a combination of military and political services; while his Indian administration, now to be described, is not the least eventful chapter in the history of that country.

CHAPTER IV

The Voyage to India

1844

One of the characteristics of Sir H. Hardinge was a resolution to carry through without delay whatever duty devolved upon him. Having therefore arranged to proceed at once to Calcutta *viâ* Marseilles and the Mediterranean, he left England on the 12th of June, 1844. Crossing the Channel, he reached Paris and Orleans on the same day. At Orleans, as in those days the railway was unfinished, a travelling carriage was hired, and the rest of the journey was accomplished *en poste* without a halt as far as Marseilles.

Here his party, which included Colonel Wood, A.D.C., and the present writer, embarked on board H.M.S. 'Geyser,' which was waiting in the harbour. After a voyage of eight days on the smooth waters of the Mediterranean, the low shore and palm-trees of Alexandria hove in sight. On disembarking, the usual hubbub of Arabs and donkey boys assailed us. We were compelled to force our way through the crowd, in order to reach the hotel. It was Sunday, and with that observance of the day which he never omitted, Sir H. Hardinge attended service at the small Protestant church in the town.

Having to deliver a despatch to Mehemet Ali from Lord Aberdeen, he repaired to the palace later in the day, and was ushered into the hall of audience. In a letter to his wife he describes the scene in these words :—'At the end of the presence chamber there sat an old man rather short and lame. He scrambled off his ottoman, walking half-way down the room to receive me. Pipes and coffee for His Highness and his brother Viceroy were then produced, all his courtiers being kept standing; and then Artin Bey, whom you may recollect in England, interpreted my limping French into Turkish. The eyes of this old man are very fine and inquisitive; he never took them off me; encouraged me to talk, but said little in reply. I then left Lord Aberdeen's despatch with the Minister, and took my leave.' Such was the portrait of this eminent man.

The next morning the conversation was resumed. The Pasha remarked that up to the age of forty-seven he was unable to read or write, but had subsequently taught himself Arabic. He always consoled himself for every misfortune by the reflection that it was so predestined, or that the loss was a real gain. Thus he praised Lord Palmerston for combining against him to deprive him of Syria and Arabia, saying that these campaigns had required 50,000 men; that the expense was thrown on Egypt; and that when Syria was forced from him by England and the Allied Powers, there was no disgrace in his son Ibrahim's abandoning it, whereby he was able to administer the finances of

Egypt at less cost and with greater benefit to the country.

On the morning of the 26th of June the Pasha's carriages conveyed us to the Mahmudiyeh Canal, where a flat-bottomed steamer was waiting for us. This canal had been made twenty years before by 300,000 poor villagers, and it is calculated that its construction cost the lives of 20,000 men. Then began a tedious journey up its waters, the shallowness of which made our progress so slow that at the first station a regiment 600 strong was ordered to tow the steamer up the muddy and sluggish stream. Our rate of progress had been about six miles an hour. The troops, who hitherto had towed the steamer from the bank, were now ordered to throw off their clothing and accoutrements; they then dashed into the water, and with long ropes dragged it up the stream. Their officers seemed to look upon them as mere animals, and treated them as such. Some fell out and were seen to fall on their knees in prayer, while the rest were urged on with those wild cries peculiar to Eastern nations. Sir Henry remarks on this:—'The same devotions were constantly going on on board, and I never was so much struck with an exhibition of religious feeling as that which seemed to have such complete possession over these poor Muhammadans.'

Cairo was reached on the evening of the 28th of June, the voyage having occupied thirty-eight hours instead of thirty. The next day the usual visit of ceremony was paid to Ibrahim Pasha, a tall, Jewish-looking man, very different in appearance from his father. There were marble courts with fountains of different designs, some constructed on the model of the Alhambra, with lions spouting out water. When Sir Henry remarked that these courts reminded him of the Alhambra, Ibrahim asked in what part of the world such a palace was situated. 'He had never heard of the Caliphs in Spain, and seemed astonished at my admiration; but when he was told that we owed the invention of the watch to the Moors, his look of incredulity was quite a study.' Ibrahim had distinguished himself in the Syrian campaign, and was now devoted to planting trees and irrigating the land by hydraulic power. He and his father were Albanians by birth, it being the tradition of the country that Turks should not be employed in the highest offices of the state.

Cairo is now well known to the European traveller. Boulevards, with gas lamps, have superseded many of its beautiful old buildings. In 1844 there was only one small hotel in the city, the Overland Route being then in its infancy. We traversed the city on horseback, with an Egyptian escort in front to clear the way. The citadel was next visited, and we were shown the spot where a single Mameluke alone escaped from the general massacre ordered by Mehemet Ali. At nine that evening we turned into bed, half-dressed, having made arrangements to ride across the desert to view the Pyramids by moonlight. I cannot do better than describe this expedition in Sir Henry's own words:—

'The night was lovely: a full moon, with the Pyramids seen indistinctly on the horizon. We had six or seven men with long poles, with a covered iron grating at the top, in which were placed pieces of dry wood to serve as torches. These men were distributed along the road, running at the rate of four or five miles an hour. The neighing of forty horses, the screams of the camels, the partial obscurity and conflict between the light of the moon and that of the large torches, contributed to make it one of the most extraordinary scenes I had ever witnessed. I am as fresh as when I started, having ridden twenty-four miles there and back.'

On our return to Cairo, our farewell interview with Ibrahim took place. He insisted on giving us a Turkish dinner; and it was strange to see four officers booted and spurred reclining on ottomans, with picturesque attendants to hand round the dishes, no knives and forks being allowed, only chopsticks. Ibrahim himself tore up with his fingers the meat which was placed before him, whilst sherbet and other cooling drinks washed down this Eastern fare.

After taking our final leave, we got into an English landau driven by an Englishman, with a postillion on the leaders, and horsed by animals of the country. After the usual amount of neighing and kicking we at last got under weigh. There were relays of Nubian runners carrying torches as usual, going at the rate of twelve miles an hour. When we had galloped in this style about fifty miles, changing horses at every ten, the unfortunate postillion, who had determined to ride the whole way (eighty-four miles), was thrown under the carriage by his horse falling. We feared he was killed, but it turned out that his foot was only bruised. We left him at the next bungalow, consoling him with a present.

In the words of Sir Henry, 'We then went the remainder of the distance with four-in-hand, the Englishman driving with extraordinary skill and speed. Suez was reached an hour after sunrise, the distance between Cairo and the latter place having occupied only twelve hours. I stopped and dressed in the same room that Napoleon had used during his campaign in Egypt; and, our boats being ready, I was on board the "Hindostan" for breakfast. The heat was intense, 94° in our cabins, while in the engine-room it was, of course, almost insupportable (120°). In carrying on their duties the unfortunate stokers are obliged, in order to keep body and soul together, to drink strong spirits. Their wages are high, but their lives are short.'

Such was the Egypt of those days. The country has since passed through many vicissitudes. It was a dream of Lord Ellenborough to bring about its occupation by British troops; and there is a letter from him in existence in which he expresses the desire to have Sir H. Hardinge as Commander-in-

Chief in India, in order that they might conjointly carry out such a project.

On the 1st of July we were steaming down the Red Sea, and on the 5th disembarked at Aden, which was carefully inspected by Sir Henry. Mounting his horse before daybreak, he rode over the whole cantonment, after having first inspected H.M.'s 17th Foot and the 47th Regiment of Madras Native Infantry. He remarks in a letter to his wife that this chaotic mass of volcanic rock, with hardly a blade of grass visible, exceeded anything he had ever seen in Europe or America. The Arabs of the neighbourhood were small, active men; but when he went down the ranks of his own sturdy Englishmen, their marked superiority over the Sepoys of the garrison was a matter of no small satisfaction to him. During his short stay at Aden he made notes on all the weak points of defence then to be detected, and on his return to the steamer employed himself in drawing up an official report pointing out the errors of the Bombay Engineers, and proving how unnecessary was the extravagant expenditure then going on upon the rock.

This Aden report, the substance of which was made public, is considered to be among the ablest of Lord Hardinge's military minutes. Though not himself a military engineer, he had acquired at the Staff College all the information requisite for seizing at once upon the strong and weak points of such a question. He ridiculed the idea of making Aden a

Gibraltar, while Singapore, Hong Kong, and the Cape remained practically defenceless. He laid down the principle that works for 1200 men in peace and 1500 in war were sufficient protection against any enemy that was not master of the sea. I may here mention that such was the confidence reposed in him on these questions that, soon after his return from India, Lord John Russell asked him, although not then in office, to draw up a scheme for fortifying our coasts and detailing the number of ships he deemed necessary for home defence.

In another fortnight our party reached Point de Galle. Twenty-four hours sufficed for coaling; so that after dining with the Governor of Ceylon, an old Peninsular officer, we were again at sea. At Madras we lay to for a few hours, surrounded by those catamarans which defy the heaviest surf. Then, with a fair wind, we reached the Sand Heads at the mouth of the Húglí on the 23rd of July. On approaching Calcutta, Lord Ellenborough's private secretary, Captain H. M. Durand, came on board. Captain Durand was on Lord Ellenborough's departure appointed Governor of the Tenasserim Provinces, and subsequently made his mark as Sir Henry Durand in the annals of Indian history.

The reception of a new Governor-General on the steps of Government House, although an accustomed ceremonial in the eyes of the Calcutta world, is a novel and imposing sight for European travellers. Lord Ellenborough and his Council met the new

Governor-General in the Marble Hall of Government House, this reception being followed by a State dinner, which the civil and military dignitaries attended. Sir Henry Hardinge was then sworn in, and on the following day entered upon those laborious duties to which he devoted unwearied zeal and energy for more than three years.

CHAPTER V

First Year at Calcutta

1844–45

Lord Hardinge always expressed himself deeply grateful for the advice and help so heartily rendered to him by the members of the Indian services, both civil and military. And it is only just to record the names of those who formed his Council at Calcutta, and of those who were at this time at the head of the several departments of the Secretariat. Sir Hugh Gough, a Peninsular officer somewhat senior to Sir Henry Hardinge, was commander-in-chief. The military member of Council was Sir George Pollock, who had shortly before returned from leading the army of Kábul through the Khäibar Pass. The legal member of Council, appointed in England, was Charles Hay Cameron, a pupil of Bentham; the representatives of the civil service were Sir Herbert Maddock and Frederick Millett. The foreign secretary was Currie (afterwards Sir Frederick), with W. Edwards for his assistant; the home department was under Bushby, finance under Dorin. The administration of Bengal was under the direct charge of the Governor-General, with Halliday for his secretary; though when Sir H. Hardinge was called to the frontier, Sir

Herbert Maddock officiated as Lieutenant-Governor. The sole survivors (1890) are W. Edwards and Sir Frederick Halliday; the latter recently retired from the India Council, after a long and distinguished service of more than sixty years.

It was the Governor-General's custom, after a short ride at daybreak, to transact the current business of the day with the different members of the Secretariat. He was recommended not to grant interviews. Had he done so, it would have been impossible, ruling as he then did Lower Bengal as well as the whole of India, to have got through his day's work. There was hardly an official at Government House who did not recognise the necessity of this principle.

Once installed in office, Sir H. Hardinge spared no opportunity of enquiring without delay into the military departments of the country. Having devoted so much of his time and energy during his English career to questions of military organisation and national defences, he felt, as he remarks in a letter written at this period, that, although he wished to maintain the Sikh Government in power and not to enlarge our overgrown empire, due precautions must be observed. Troops were moved up quietly towards the frontier, so that when the crisis came he was equal to the occasion.

While these precautionary measures were going on almost unobserved, the Governor-General by no means neglected such matters of civil administration as called for special attention.

The *Calcutta Review* of 1847 remarks that 'The Punjab has been called the difficulty of recent administrations, but Oudh is the difficulty of all.' Such a difficulty now arose from the King of Oudh's attempt to supplant his Wazír, Muna-ud Daula, by a mere upstart, Amin-ud Daula. The Governor-General might have enforced one of the articles of the Treaty, but preferred giving friendly advice accompanied by a solemn warning, which for the time put an end to the systematic disregard of the Resident's representations. It was reserved to him at a later period of his administration, on visiting Lucknow, to take up the question from a more serious point of view.

The next subject that engaged his attention was that of native education, which may be regarded as a test by which to measure the beneficent results of British administration in India. The Muhammadan College at Calcutta and the Hindu Sanskrit College at Benares (in addition to the missionary and other private institutions) had already done much good by introducing improved literature and modifying the prejudices of the higher classes of the population. Education—and especially education in English—has since advanced by rapid strides, until what was at that time but a small beginning, has now grown into a general system of instruction, with ramifications in every village.

To stimulate this progress was the aim of Sir Henry Hardinge's Minute, dated October 10th, 1844: 'The Governor-General, having taken into consideration the existing state of education in Bengal, and being of opinion that it is highly desirable to afford it every reasonable encouragement by holding out to those who have taken advantage of the opportunity of instruction a fair prospect of employment in the public service, and thereby not only to reward individual merit, but to enable the State to profit as largely as possible by the result of the measures adopted of late years for the instruction of the people as well by the Government as by private individuals and societies, has resolved that in every possible case a preference shall be given in the selection of candidates for public employment to those who have been educated in the institutions thus established, and especially to those who have distinguished themselves therein by a more than ordinary degree of merit.'

The effect of this Minute was remarkable. Early in the December following, the Calcutta Babus called a meeting, at which five hundred native gentlemen attended, to present an address to the Governor-General in acknowledgment of the policy he had propounded. In his reply, Sir Henry Hardinge dwelt on the advantages both to the governors and to the governed of the spread of education, laying special stress on the services of natives of superior intelligence as tending to the happiness and prosperity of the community at large.

In the following March (1845) the Governor-General distributed the prizes at the Hindu and Muhammadan Colleges, and was much struck by the ability of the native students, remarking how admirably they delivered some of Shakespeare's finest speeches, and how on examination they explained with intelligence and fluency the passages which they had recited. He concluded his address by giving his hearers a practical account of the magic powers of steam and electricity, and announced amid cheers the appointment of one of the students as a deputy-magistrate for special proficiency in the English language.

The seed thus sown has borne good fruit. Not only has the native youth come forward to compete with English students in examinations in England, but in every Council in India native representatives now take their seats by the side of their English colleagues, thereby adding weight and stability to our institutions.

Almost contemporaneously with this Education Minute, the Governor-General issued another notification of special interest to the poorer classes of the community. This was a reduction of the salt duty, which was at that time levied on different principles and at different rates in the three Presidencies. The reduction applied only to Bengal, where the supply of salt was then chiefly derived from a Government monopoly of manufacture, somewhat similar to the existing opium system, although importation from England, which has now almost entirely superseded this local manufacture, had even then begun. At that time the rate of duty in Bengal was three and a-quarter rupees per *maund* (80 lbs.), contrasting with three-quarters of a rupee in Bombay and one rupee in Madras. Lord Hardinge struck off the odd fraction, bringing the duty in Bengal down to three rupees.

This is not the place to consider the incidence of the salt-tax, which has frequently formed a subject for discussion in the Imperial Parliament as well as in India. Suffice it to say, that it forms the one impost which every inhabitant of the country must pay; and that, from the nature of the case, it falls with special severity upon the poorest classes. It was this consideration that influenced Sir H. Hardinge in sanctioning the reduction. It had previously been contemplated while Mr. W. Wilberforce Bird was Deputy-Governor of Bengal; but had then been postponed through fear of tampering with a branch of the revenue which yielded more than two millions sterling in Bengal alone. The reduction of one quarter of a rupee per *maund* was estimated to produce a loss of about £120,000.

Seldom has a just financial policy been followed by more favourable results. The reduced rate was originally guaranteed until April, 1849. But before that time arrived, Sir Henry's military reductions after the close of the Sikh War had so much improved the Indian finances that he was able to give up a further quarter of a rupee in 1847, and to leave it to his successor to make a similar reduction again in 1849. The varying rates of the salt-tax were not finally equalised until 1882, when a uniform duty of two rupees per *maund* was fixed for the whole of India.

Although to Lord Dalhousie belongs the credit, which cannot be over-estimated, of having founded that vast system of railway communication now existing in India, it is but fair to mention the steps taken by his predecessor with reference to this important question. Having made himself well acquainted with the various reports laid before him, Sir Henry Hardinge drew up a Minute on which a writer in the *Calcutta Review* makes the following comments:—'We are much mistaken if his Excellency has ever written a State paper on which he can reflect with more satisfaction, or which will more worthily illustrate his sagacity, penetration, and practical wisdom as a statesman.'

In this Minute, Sir H. Hardinge gave his approval to the Grand Trunk Line (now the East Indian Railway), as offering special advantages on military, political, and commercial grounds. With regard to the question of land, he argued that it should be granted free to the companies; and he further maintained that the assistance to be given by the State should include other substantial concessions, on the ground that English capitalists would not enter into such speculations without more encouragement from the Government. In his opinion, the reasons for such assistance arose from the military and political advantages to be derived from the lines when completed. He argued too in this Minute that it would not be prudent to leave the whole affair in the hands of the Government—the State in India, as in England, deriving its advantage without interfering with the profits of the companies. The Court of Directors at that time entertained grave doubts whether an extensive railway system was applicable to India. Various lines were competing for precedence, and neither the Court nor the Government appeared to have sufficient information on the general question.

Mr. Sims, well known in the scientific world, assisted by two officers of the Bengal Engineers, drew up an exhaustive report on the question. Lines were surveyed. The practicability of bridging over the Soane (Son) River, with other works of importance, was duly considered. The land question was so far settled that the Home authorities decided that the land should be given free to the companies, since its purchase could be effected by the Government more easily than by individual companies. The President of the Council (Sir Herbert Maddock) suggested that at the end of twenty-five years the railways should revert to the State, on a fair valuation, and that no dividend should be guaranteed either before or after the completion of the work, one-tenth of the capital being paid to the State in the event of failure.

It will be seen from the foregoing that, although Sir Henry Hardinge's attention was concentrated in a great measure on the North-West Frontier and the affairs of the Punjab, he found time to study and grapple with such a difficult and comprehensive subject as that of Indian railways. Years have passed since these deliberations took place. Some of the principles which he enunciated have been carried out, and England has conferred on India a boon of inestimable value; while the facility of rapid communication has enabled the State to reduce its armies, to provide security for the population against famine, and to place its political relations on a much firmer basis.

It was in the summer of the year 1844 that the little war in Kolhápur and Sáwantwári occurred. Prompt measures suppressed the insurrection; and Sir Henry Hardinge at once approved of the appointment of Colonel Outram, who brought the affair to a speedy termination. The entire authority in the State of Kolhápur was vested in British agents during the minority of the young Rájá. The country soon became perfectly tranquil. The forts were dismantled and the hereditary militia disbanded; while due punishment was inflicted on the leaders of the insurrection.

Another subject which required the attention of Sir Henry Hardinge during the first year of his rule was the prevalence of human sacrifice among the Kandhs, or Kondhs. This wild tribe, occupying the hill tracts on the borders of Orissa and Ganjám, had just been brought under effectual British supervision. The British officers ascertained that the Kandhs were addicted to the practice of offering human victims, 'bought with a price,' to the Earth-god, in order to propitiate his favour at seed-time and harvest. By an Act of the Legislative Council (Act XXI. of 1845) a special agency was established for the tract of country inhabited by the Kandhs; and this horrible custom was suppressed by the energetic interference of a series of able officers, among whom Major Macpherson is deserving of special mention.

Before he left Calcutta for the frontier, the Governor-General also passed an Order prohibiting Sunday labour—a boon to all creeds, and one that was thoroughly appreciated by every section of the community. This rule has been consistently carried out in Government works, factories, and all official undertakings. It means a weekly day of rest to hundreds of thousands who would not otherwise have had one.

CHAPTER VI

ANARCHY AT LAHORE: PREPARATIONS FOR WAR

WE must now turn to the state of affairs on the North-West Frontier. It has been said that the pages of Gibbon do not contain a chapter more full of horrors than those which were of daily occurrence at the Court of Lahore. After the death of Ranjít Singh, intrigue, debauchery, and riot reigned supreme. Rájás and Ministers alike were massacred in quick succession; while the army of the Khálsa, like the praetorians of Imperial Rome, sold the supreme power, which rested entirely in their hands, to the highest bidder. They had expelled their officers, including two French generals, Avitable and Court, and transacted all negotiations by means of Pancháyats or representative committees.

Ranjít Singh is described as spending his last days on a bed, scarcely able to speak, but still dictating his orders to his officers. The road from Lahore to the temple at Jawálamúkhi[1] in the Jálandhar Doáb was dotted with hackeries filled with ghee to feed the sacred flame and propitiate the Deity, till one morning in 1839 it was announced that the 'Lion's' spirit had fled to another world.

[1] A model in bronze of the silver gates of this Temple, copied for Lord Hardinge, is now at South Park, Penshurst.

When Sir Henry Hardinge arrived in India, both the Rájá Sher Singh, a son of Ranjít, and also the Minister Dhián Singh, a brother of Ghuláb Singh, had recently been murdered on the same day. By means of bribes to the army, Híra Singh, a son of Dhián, obtained the succession to the post of Minister; while the infant Dhulíp, another son of Ranjít, was placed on the throne, with his mother, the Rání, as Queen-Regent. Híra Singh is thus described by Sir Henry Hardinge:—'He is the handsomest man in the East, twenty-four years of age, and has shown considerable ability. He is brave and reckless, and it is probable that among people so ferocious he will not long escape a violent death.' . . . 'Of the chief Sardárs, ten have already been destroyed; and when the expected event of Híra Singh's death takes place, some soldier of energy may possibly be found capable of controlling this turbulent army.' The same letter also contains a description of Ghuláb Singh:—'The most remarkable man in the country is Ghuláb Singh, the uncle of Híra Singh. He was formerly a running footman in Ranjít's service. Entrusted with the task of conquering the Hill tribes, he displayed great military ability and secured for himself a revenue exceeding £600,000 a year.'

At this time Kashmír was in a state of insurrection. The Afgháns were threatening Pesháwar, while Híra Singh was endeavouring to induce Ghuláb Singh to march against them. The Governor of Múltán had lately been in conflict with the troops of the Sikh Darbár, so that the Punjab was threatened from various quarters, and its dismemberment seemed inevitable. The next event was the death of Híra Singh and Pandit Julla, the latter one of the ablest and most astute of the Lahore Sardárs. They both fell in an action which took place on December 21st, 1844.

Peshora Singh was now made use of by the army to coerce the Ráni. They declared him to be their Sovereign, but he declined the proffered honour. Major Broadfoot, the British Agent, at once informed the Darbár that the Governor-General had recognised Dhulíp Singh as the Sovereign, and would be no party to permitting any other successor to Ranjít. In the meantime, overtures were made to our Agent by the Darbár. They asked for a British force to be permanently stationed at Lahore, with the view of overawing the army. But Major Broadfoot again declined to interfere. The Governor-General remarks in a letter written at this time, 'That as long as this military power is under no control, there is no chance of a permanent government; that the Government of India were determined to respect the Treaty of 1809, and to avoid all interference with the dissensions of the Darbár.'

The Pancháyats now entered into negotiations with Ghuláb Singh. He received them with humility, placing his sword and shield at their feet, and gave £250,000 to be distributed among the men. The post of Minister was offered to him; which, with his usual cunning, he declined in favour of Peshora Singh. Negotiations were broken off; but the crafty

Ghuláb again appeared, in a white sheet, expressing sorrow for what had taken place. He threw himself on the mercy of the Pancháyats, who in consequence of his promises of higher pay swore allegiance to him as Minister. Meanwhile, the Rání had caused Peshora Singh to be murdered at Lahore, through the agency of her favourite Lál Singh and her brother Jowahir Singh, the latter of whom was appointed Minister. But he did not long hold that office. Having been called to account by the delegates of the army for the murder of Peshora Singh, he was shot down on his elephant, after the infant Mahárájá had been torn from his side and conveyed to a place of safety. Four of Jowahir Singh's widows were burnt on the funeral pile, whilst the Rání prostrated herself before them.

The army was now divided in allegiance between Lál Singh and another Sardár named Tej Singh; while Ghuláb Singh hung back as usual, waiting on events. On the 4th of December, 1845, affairs became critical. The Rání, foreseeing that another revolution would be fatal to her, ordered the army to march to the Sutlej, which then formed the British boundary. When they asked, 'What had the English done, that their territory was to be invaded?' she replied that the whole of the English Sepoys would join them at once. Then followed the usual recriminations, with mutual accusations of treachery. But the end was at hand. In a few days the first shot had been fired, and this unprovoked aggression startled even those who had long looked upon it as inevitable.

It is the lot of public men, whether soldiers or statesmen, to have their actions closely scanned and canvassed. Of course, there were those who, during the interval that elapsed between the battles of Múdkí and Firozsháh and the crowning victory of Sobráon, maintained that due preparations had not been made against the emergency and that the Governor-General had been taken by surprise. A writer in the *Quarterly Review* of June, 1846, undertook the task of giving an historical account of the events of this period. Unfortunately, many of his facts and figures were inaccurate, not from any wish on the part of the author (who was, indeed, an old friend of Sir Henry Hardinge) to detract from his merits, but from insufficiency of information and incorrectness of details.

The words of the Reviewer are these:—'If there had been urgent arguments addressed to Lord Ellenborough in favour of a peaceful reign, the wish both of the Court of Directors and of the Cabinet on that head was expressed to Sir Henry Hardinge with increased earnestness. Sir Henry entered upon the duties of his office more anxious than perhaps any other Governor-General had been before him to signalise the entire term of his residence in India by the useful labours of peace. At the same time, he did not consider himself bound either to censure or retrace the steps which his predecessor might have taken in an opposite direction. He found the attention of Lord Ellenborough had been turned seriously towards the North-Western Frontier; that all towns from Delhi to Karnál were filled with troops; that the Commander-in-Chief had already surveyed the whole extent of the Protected States with a view to make choice of military positions, and that the advanced posts of Ludhiána and Firozpur had been strengthened. *Sir H. Hardinge neither undid anything of all this*, nor found fault with it, but he carefully abstained from the discussion in Council or elsewhere of topics which might turn men's thoughts to war.'

Again, 'That he kept his eye on the Punjab, and was neither regardless of the confusion which its affairs were falling into nor of the consequences to which this might possibly lead, is most certain. He had already directed the works at Ludhiána and Firozpur to be strengthened, and raised the garrison of the latter place from 4000 to 7000 men. The former was held by about 6000; and at Ambála, where Gough's head-quarters were established, and among the cantonments in the rear, there were about 7500 of all arms. But as Sir Henry certainly did not anticipate that the whole power of the Punjab would be thrown across the Sutlej, he naturally concluded that there was force enough at hand to meet and repel whatever invasion might be hazarded.'

The apologetic tone of these extracts seems to imply that Lord Ellenborough had prepared everything and Lord Hardinge nothing. So far from the towns from Delhi to Karnál being filled with troops, Lord Ellenborough had abolished Karnál as a military station; and as for the other towns, there was hardly a soldier in them.

The writer in the *Quarterly*, when called upon by Sir Henry Hardinge to amend his facts and figures, as well as the conclusions he had arrived at, published a 'Note' in the January number of the year following based upon information sent from Simla, having been requested to lay the real facts before the public. The contents of this 'Note' may be described as the Governor-General's 'case.' He was naturally annoyed at having been misrepresented in a periodical so widely read and of such weight, and it is with this view that the details of his military preparations are now given upon his own authority.

Now, let us see how the case really stood:

Post.	Strength as left by Lord Ellenborough.	Strength at first breaking out of War.	Increased preparation made by Lord Hardinge.
Firozpur	4596 men 12 guns	10472 men 24 guns	5876 men 12 guns
Ludhiána	3030 men 12 guns	7235 men 12 guns	4205 men 0 guns
Ambála	4113 men 24 guns	12972 men 32 guns	8859 men 8 guns
Meerut	5873 men 18 guns	9844 men 26 guns	3971 men 8 guns
Whole Frontier, exclusive of Hill Stations which remained the same	17612 men 66 guns	40523 men 94 guns	22911 men 28 guns

The above return, which was drawn up by the Governor-General at the time, speaks for itself. He landed in India in July, 1844. On the 23rd August of that year he addressed the Commander-in-Chief on the distribution of the force in Bengal. On the 8th September, five Native regiments were placed at the disposal of the Commander-in-Chief for distribution between Meerut and the frontier. On the 11th of the same month, confidential orders were sent for the construction of two barracks at Firozpur, to accommodate a regiment of European infantry and two batteries of artillery. The two European regiments at Sabáthu and Kasauli were also added to the garrison. In January, 1845, the Bombay Government was requested to send up H.M.'s 14th Light Dragoons to the frontier, and the batteries in the Sirhind Division were raised from 90 to 130 horses. As the result of these measures, the British force at and above Ambála was augmented from 13,600 men and 48 guns in January, 1844, to 32,500 men and 68 guns in December, 1845; while the total force at and above Meerut, including Delhi and the Hill Stations, which had been only 24,000 men and 66 guns, now amounted to 45,500 men and 98 guns.

Lord Ellenborough had made no fresh distribution of troops before leaving India, but he had ordered fifty-six boats to be built on the Indus. These Sir Henry Hardinge brought up to Firozpur in September, 1845, and on them, immediately after the battle of Sobráon, the army crossed the river

Sutlej. Pontoons had likewise been brought up from Sind, and on the same occasion 24,000 men were conveyed across the river, besides a siege train of 40 heavy guns, 100,000 camp-followers, and 68,000 baggage-animals. In the Memorandum referred to, the Governor-General observes that 'The result of these arrangements was that, nine days after the Sikhs had crossed the Sutlej, the British army fought the battle of Firozsháh, 19,700 strong, with 65 guns, including seven regiments of British infantry, a force unparalleled in the annals of India.' 'It may be asked why the force at and above Ambála only fought 19,000 strong at Firozsháh. The answer is, that if in nine days 19,000 men and 65 guns out of a total force of 32,000 men were available, with a reserve of 7090 men and 24 guns marching up from Meerut, the Governor-General had done all that wisdom and foresight could have achieved.'

The writer in the *Quarterly Review* makes another misstatement when he writes that 'The Commander-in-Chief, conceiving hostilities about to commence, ordered up to Meerut a regiment of European cavalry and two of infantry; but various causes connected with the political state of affairs induced the Governor-General to disapprove of the latter suggestion.' And further he adds that 'This forward movement was countermanded by the Governor-General, and our preparations may be said to have reverted to what they were in the summer.'

The answer to all this is a simple negative. *No*

regiments from Meerut were ordered to march by the Commander-in-Chief, with the exception of the 9th Lancers. The regiments there were only ordered to hold themselves in readiness. The Governor-General wrote to the Commander-in-Chief: 'I concur in moving up the 4th and 8th Irregular Cavalry with the wing of the Shaikháwati Brigade. With regard to H.M.'s 9th Lancers and the Sirmur Battalion, I have forwarded the Adjutant-General's letter postponing their march; agreeing with you, however, in the orders at the time they were issued. The force at and in front of Ambála must be strong enough to move on Firozpur without waiting for the force at Meerut. My own impression remains unaltered. When I hear of a single piece of artillery having crossed the Sutlej, I shall consider the movement to be made in earnest.' The Commander-in-Chief concurred and observed: 'I am still of opinion that they never will be beaten this side of the river, except as plunderers.'

It is unnecessary to make further observations on these extracts. They prove that the Governor-General countermanded no orders of the Commander-in-Chief, except as regards the 9th Lancers; and they also show that the Commander-in-Chief himself did not expect the Sikh invasion, and considered that there was no necessity for moving up the Meerut force.

The Governor-General arrived at Ambála on the 3rd December, 1845. On the 6th, Sir J. Littler asked for another European regiment at Firozpur. The Governor-General approved, and recorded his opinion that the Ambála force should be moved up immediately. With regard to Firozpur he observes: 'My views have always been expressed and recorded that the force there should be increased, and I am therefore very glad to have my opinions supported by the Commander-in-Chief.' On the 10th December, H.M.'s 80th Foot was ordered to march on Firozpur, and two Native regiments were moved up from the rear. On the 7th the Commander-in-Chief writes: 'The force shall be all closed up as you wish, giving the Darbár full time for decision.' It appears from this that the Commander-in-Chief was well aware that the Governor-General was only waiting for the final answer to his letter of the 3rd December, when the Vakíl was dismissed. On the 9th the Governor-General ordered H.M.'s 29th Foot and the 1st Bengal Europeans from the Hills to be in readiness to march. Sir J. Littler was now perfectly satisfied with the strength of this force, and wrote that if the Sikhs attacked him he was quite prepared to receive them.

On the 12th December the Commander-in-Chief moved from Ambála, whilst the Governor-General rode over to inspect Ludhiána. Deeming it secure, he gave orders for the withdrawal of its garrison to Basián, the great grain depôt on which the army depended for its supplies. This movement was one of the most important in the whole campaign. Had Basián been destroyed by any sudden inroad of plunderers, the army would have been delayed by at least ten days, and Firozpur itself might have been cut off[1]. On the 15th the main body of the army was disencumbered of its baggage, while their commissariat-elephants brought up the stores and the footsore men of the two regiments who had come from the Hills.

It has been necessary to enter into the above details because Sir Henry Hardinge felt very strongly on the question which had been raised. The result showed his foresight. In the three subsequent actions not a man could have been spared; in the last, every available soldier was utilised. His case was proved and his defence is complete.

It may be well to insert here the latest intelligence from the Lahore Darbár, which was received daily by Major Broadfoot, who had now joined the camp of the Governor-General:—'Tej Singh, on the Rání's urging him to move forward, said they had none of their old leaders left. They knew that certain death was before them, and refused to march. Ghuláb Singh, on the other hand, was ready to treat, saying that he would carry out whatever orders might be given by the British Government. Bhai Rám Singh was also deputed by him to negotiate with the British.' So that up to the last there was positive doubt as to the intentions of the Darbár.

[1] In this step the Governor-General acted on his own responsibility. The Commander-in-Chief had protested against the evacuation of Ludhiána on the score of its exposure to hostile attacks. But the Governor-General saw the absolute necessity of placing 5000 men in advance of Ambála, and the result more than justified the risk he had incurred.

CHAPTER VII

Múdkí and Firozsháh

On December 12th, 1845, the Governor-General, who was two marches ahead of the Commander-in-Chief, received trustworthy intelligence that the Sikh army had crossed the Sutlej. He immediately issued a proclamation, declaring the Cis-Sutlej States to be annexed to the British territories, and calling upon the chiefs of those States for co-operation and fidelity. He then met the Commander-in-Chief, when orders were at once issued for a forced march to Esru, the object being to reach Basián before any Sikh force could destroy the stores which had been accumulated there. The Ludhiána force, 5000 strong, was in advance, while Sir J. Littler moved out of Firozpur with two brigades, to engage a considerable force of Sikhs who were threatening the town and who retired immediately. Lál Singh then advanced with the main body of the Sikh army to Firozsháh, where he entrenched himself. Afterwards, thinking possibly that the British advanced guard was only the Ludhiána force, he moved on the 18th to Múdkí, where was fought the opening battle of the campaign.

No one who has not witnessed a night march with

an Indian army can form any conception of the weird aspect of such a scene. The expiring fires round which the shivering camp-followers congregate, the roaring of the camels, the babel of tongues, the heavy tramp of the troops as they move off, form incidents that cannot be found together in any other army. The number of camp-followers, too, is legion, while the dark forms of the elephant-contingents add a mysterious character to this moving mass of dusky warriors. As the day breaks, the scene changes. The long lines of camels, the troops in column of route, the grey-headed Subahdár and the light-hearted ensign, all remind us that we are in India. Though many battle-scenes have been depicted in Europe, India for many reasons is to the artist a sealed book. No country is so fertile in picturesque incident, none so glorious in colour and atmospheric effect.

It was on such a morning that the army marched to Wadní on December 16th. Sir Harry Smith was in command of the leading Division, when it was reported that the Sikhs had moved forward with the object of cutting off our supplies. The report was, to a certain extent, correct; for on arriving under the walls of the fort at Wadní, resistance was threatened and grain refused. This was but for a moment. The Horse Artillery, with their horsehair helmets and heavy jack-boots, were sent to the front, and, unlimbering, were about to open fire, when discretion proved the better part of valour, and the supplies were forthcoming. The fort, however, still held out;

and as the heavy guns had not yet been brought up, the First and Second Divisions were ordered to resume their march on the following morning, leaving it to the rear-guard to put down further resistance. Here the Governor-General gave up three hundred camels and sixty elephants, transferring all his baggage-animals to the Commissariat for the conveyance of stores and supplies. On December 17th a short march was made to Charak, and the next day a march of twenty-one miles brought the whole force to Múdkí.

According to modern ideas of the use of cavalry, our available force of that arm should have been more actively employed in scouting, &c.; and this has given rise to the criticism that the army was surprised at Múdkí. Lál Singh had taken up his position in rear of a jungle, where he was apparently waiting to be attacked. Sir Hugh Gough's despatch as Commander-in-Chief accurately describes the action, while two articles in the *Calcutta Review*, by Herbert Edwardes and Henry Lawrence, supply graphic details of this first encounter with the forces of the Khálsa.

As related in Major W. Broadfoot's Life of his distinguished brother, while we were sitting in a small tent the latter rushed in, exclaiming, 'The Sikhs are on us!' Then there was the usual stampede. Sepoys, disencumbered of their belts and cooking their 'chapatis,' picketed horses, camels but a short time before relieved of their loads, all were got together in more or less confusion. But discipline soon evolved order out of chaos. The brigades were then formed into column, and ere long a round-shot or two told us the battle had began.

Sir Hugh Gough, with the Cavalry Division, had moved to the right, and soon engaged the enemy's horse. Then ensued a sort of Balaclava mêlée, except that the Sikhs made a more determined stand than did the Russians against Scarlett's Heavy Brigade. In his official despatch, the Commander-in-Chief states that, 'whilst our twelve battalions formed from échelon of brigades into line, a heavy cannonade was opened on our advancing troops. Then the British cavalry turned the left of the Sikh army. The enemy's ample and extended line, from their superiority of numbers, far outflanked ours, but was counteracted by the flank movements of the cavalry; so that when the attack of the infantry commenced, the whole Sikh force was driven from position after position with great slaughter. Night only saved them from worse disaster, for this stout conflict was maintained during an hour and a-half of dim starlight, amidst a cloud of dust from the sandy plain, which yet more obscured every object.'

I can attest the accuracy of this description. The scene of the action was enveloped in a sort of November fog, making it difficult to distinguish friend from foe. The Governor-General, with true instinct, had been bringing into action the several infantry brigades. All his aides-de-camp had been told off to head-quarters, including Captain Arthur

Hardinge. Broadfoot, with Cust, the Assistant Political Agent, and myself alone remained. On advancing towards the line of infantry which had deployed, we saw to our dismay a regiment of Native Infantry, not only firing into the air, but some of them firing right and left. Their officers seemed to have no control over them. The men had lost their heads, and I am afraid this was not the only instance; but, as usual, the steady discipline of the Europeans carried the day.

I mention this incident because Sir H. Hardinge alluded to it in a private letter to Lord Ripon: 'The men soon got under arms. We advanced through some jungle, and after a heavy cannonade and file-firing, drove our assailants back at every point, advancing about four miles from our camp and capturing seventeen guns. The darkness of the night, and the risk of the troops firing into each other, *which they did*, rendered it necessary that the pursuit should not be continued. There can be no doubt that the following reasons may have operated prejudicially upon the Native corps. The troops having been collected from various points, and constantly engaged in marching, had only been brigaded on paper. British and Sepoy regiments who have served together before, ought to be reunited whenever it is possible to do so. The troops, therefore, were not in that state of organisation and formation so essential to discipline and field movements. The brigadiers and their staff were unknown to the men, and the men to the brigadiers, while at Múdkí the confusion of the attack, combined with the facts above-noticed, had created a feeling that the army was not well in hand.'

Sir H. Hardinge always maintained the opinion that the Sepoys resembled the Portuguese, in that they had their fighting days. At the close of the campaign, when their dread of the Khálsa troops had more or less disappeared, they fought at Sobráon with a determination to efface their former unsteadiness, and vied with the Europeans in the attack on the breast-works.

The next day, December 19th, was occupied in burying the dead. We visited the field of battle in the morning. Heaped round the captured cannon, fifteen in number, lay the stalwart forms of the Sikh gunners, locked in death's last embrace. How the native reveres his guns was well exemplified. There were few that had not fallen near the pieces they worshipped. Over the field itself there was the usual mingling of the dead. The Khálsa soldier, the European linesman, the young officer, with groups of horses and camels, all lay in one shapeless mass.

The night before I had ridden back to camp in advance of the columns. I rushed to the mess tent for some water, where I found Baxu, the old Khánsamah, arranging the plates and chairs as if he was preparing for a State dinner at Government House. He had begun life with Lord Wellesley, and faithfully did he serve successive Governors-General. On that night there were several vacant chairs! Herries, the son of the Cabinet Minister, and Munro, both admirable staff officers, were killed; Hillier was severely wounded. Amongst the distinguished general officers who fell on this occasion were Sir John McCaskell, K.C.B., and Sir R. H. Sale, K.C.B., whose services were so pre-eminent and well known that it is needless to recapitulate them. After performing the last melancholy rites, it was necessary to turn to the more pressing exigencies of the situation.

The most important incident of this day was the formal offer of Sir Henry Hardinge to place his military services unreservedly at the disposal of Sir Hugh Gough the Commander-in-Chief, who suggested that he could serve in no other capacity than second in command. Sir Hugh Gough reports this in his despatch:—'This evening [the 19th] in addition to the valuable counsel with which you had in every emergency before favoured me, you were pleased yet further to strengthen my hands by kindly offering your services as second in command in my army. I need hardly say with what pleasure the offer was accepted.'

This proposal has been much criticised; but as it will be referred to again further on, it is unnecessary to dwell upon it now. Herbert Edwardes, in his account of the campaign in the *Calcutta Review*, observes: 'It has been censured as derogatory and rash. We have every respect for the abstract dignity and high mightiness of the Governor-General of India, embodying as it does the irresponsibility of the Great Mogul with the infallibility of the Pope, but we are among those who think that to lead on a wing of a British army against the enemies of this country can derogate from the dignity of no man.'

The same day, the 29th Queen's, the 1st Bengal Europeans, and two Native regiments were brought up on commissariat-elephants, which had been despatched from the camp at Múdkí. Prince Waldemar of Prussia, with his aides-de-camp Counts Grueben and Oriolla, had previously joined the army in time for the battle. Their charming manners and gallant bearing endeared them to all with whom they came in contact. At Firozsháh they were under a very heavy fire; and it was not until matters had become critical that they were specially ordered to the rear, as the Governor-General declined to be responsible for their safety.

Everything being ready by midnight on the 20th December, another night march took place. All were aware that a general action was again imminent; one of the Governor-General's staff had even predicted that every member of it would be hit, and little knew at the time that his forebodings were about to be so nearly realised. The welcome dawn of day at last disclosed the country which was about to be the scene of another sanguinary encounter. A broad expanse of level plain, dotted here and there with low jungle, was no doubt generally favourable for extended operations; but the lines of the Sikh camp had been so skilfully chosen that our troops were to a certain extent impeded in the advance by the jungle. A circuitous route was taken, with the view of attacking the weakest face of the parallelogram; and on halting we knew that it would not be long before Sir J. Littler would come up with his 5000 men and twenty-four guns.

At this moment, as the Governor-General and his staff were sharing the provisions which they had brought in their saddle-bags and holsters, Sir Hugh Gough rode up and exclaimed: 'Sir Henry, if we attack at once I promise you a splendid victory!' There was a small grove of trees some fifty yards off, to which the two generals at once retired; what there took place was for many years known only to a few, to whom it was communicated in confidence. After a long lapse of years, these incidents may now be made public. Sir Hugh proceeded to repeat his proposals, which the Governor-General in the most positive manner declined to entertain. At last, wearied out by the reiteration, he calmly observed: 'Then, Sir Hugh, I must exercise my civil powers as Governor-General, and forbid the attack until Littler's force has come up.' Such powers had never before been exercised by any Governor-General in the field. Once, in an Indian debate in the House of Lords, Lord Albemarle alluded to the fact without mentioning names, but it passed unnoticed. I mention the incident because I was an eye-witness of the scene, much speculation being rife among our staff as to the probable result of the interview under the little grove of trees.

Littler had left his camp standing, to disarm suspicion. Quietly at 8 a.m. he moved off without Tej Singh being aware of his departure. Broadfoot and his Sawárs met him, and conducted him to the Commander-in-Chief. His force arrived about 1 p.m. His route and his orders had been carefully laid down, with the entire concurrence of Sir H. Gough, so that it was with no small surprise that the Governor-General found himself confronted with such extraordinary proposals. It is almost impossible to realise what would have been the result of an attack without the substantial reinforcement of 5000 men and twenty-four guns, in addition to the strength of the Ambála force. As it turned out, the fate of India trembled in the balance during the eventful night of the 21st December [1].

Major W. Broadfoot, in the biography of his brother, mentions that some were of opinion that the attack on the Sikh camp was commenced at too late an hour of the afternoon. It will be seen from a subsequent letter that a most unaccountable delay did take place in getting the troops into position; but it was absolutely necessary to attack that day, as may be learned from the following extract from a letter of the Governor-General's to Lord Ripon, dated December 27th: 'I then informed the Commander-in-Chief that there was daylight for an action, and he made his

[1] No moment was perhaps more critical during the whole of the campaign, but the Governor-General was equal to the occasion—his firmness and decision were as important as they were characteristic of the man.

arrangements. About 3 p.m. we were formed opposite the entrenched camp, and, I think, on the weakest side, being considerably to the left of his defences raised to oppose an attack from the Múdkí road. It was scarcely possible to adopt any other alternative than to fight the battle that afternoon. Our forces were as strong as they ever would be in twenty-four hours. The men were not tired. There were three hours of daylight. No water was to be procured for so large a force within a moderate distance. If we had delayed till the next morning, our wounded might have been sacrificed at Múdkí during the night, and the town of Firozpur destroyed by Tej Singh's force in the neighbourhood. The troops were ready, and the moral effect of fighting at once prevented Tej Singh from coming up. I entirely approved of the battle being fought that evening.'

The crisis had at last arrived. The brigades were deployed into line, and advanced as steadily as the low tree jungle permitted. When they emerged on more open ground, the Sikh batteries could easily be discerned. The following letter from the pen of the Governor-General deals so graphically with what took place on that eventful evening, that it should be given *in extenso*. It is addressed to the President of the Council in Calcutta, and is dated January 5th, 1846:—

'The ground was intersected with low trees and bushes, affording cover to the timid to skulk behind, and rendering the advance in line very difficult; and when we did open into the plain, the fire from the batteries with grape and canister at 300 yards was tremendous. The Sikh guns were well served, and vigorously defended to the last. For me, therefore, who have commanded Portuguese troops, I can fairly say that they would not have behaved better than our Sepoys did, and as the list of killed and wounded will prove. The batteries were carried by our brave British infantry. Sir J. Littler told me H. M.'s 62nd gave way when almost in the battery, but what is the fact? One hundred and eighty-five men were killed and wounded in ten minutes by grape and canister, and can he or any other officer be surprised that boys who never before heard a ball whistle should turn back? Their officers were nearly annihilated, and I maintain, and shall on the first occasion tell that regiment, they nobly did their duty.

'The people under my immediate command carried the battery and camp; and we were pushing through in the midst of their tents when by the explosion of some powder or tumbrils the tents and forage caught fire, and we were obliged almost in the dark to take up ground on the edge of the burning camp. Here I insisted on every man lying down and not talking. On the left, Littler having failed by the 62nd Queen's giving way, he retired a short distance, and we could not find him. On my right I was joined in about an hour by the Commander-in-Chief. Firing was heard on our right, which we supposed to be the reserve under Sir Harry Smith, and on our left, which we supposed to be Littler. Thus the left centre having perfectly succeeded but obliged by the burning of the camp and the darkness of the night to suspend its operations, we remained quiet, the enemy on both flanks of the camp firing shot and grape in the dark, while their camp opposite to us was continually exploding live shells and loose powder. In this state we passed the night, hearing the march of large Sikh bodies close to us. Whenever they were too impudent, I ordered up Colonel Wood with the 80th and 1st Europeans. The vigour of this attack and the British cheers in carrying the battery at midnight, with the spiking of their guns, caused them, I believe, to recede and confine their firing to the batteries on their extreme flanks.

'The despondency of several brave officers was great during the night. My resolution was recorded three or four times, when they came to me with timid counsels of retreat upon Firozpur, that our line of duty was clear, namely, to wait patiently for daylight and then, without a moment's hesitation, to attack the enemy and carry everything before us that remained to be carried. Sir Hugh came to me, candidly avowed the critical state of our affairs, but most cordially concurred in all my sentiments. I sent away every officer I did not absolutely want, such as Prince Waldemar, my doctor, and Wood, who although wounded, refused to go until I ordered him off.

'When morning came, we carried battery after battery without a check, and completed the victory which the conflagration and darkness had suspended.

From about 8 to 11 a.m. and at 3 p.m. the enemy came towards us with immense bodies of cavalry and infantry. The latter showed the same spirit as before; but whenever our jaded men advanced the Sikhs retired. The 3rd Light Dragoons had in all these affairs behaved admirably. The Governor-General's body-guard [a Native cavalry corps] behaved beautifully at Múdkí as well as at Firozsháh.'

I would now quote another report of the action in a letter to Lord Ripon [1], dated December 27th. After describing the character of the advance, Sir H. Hardinge continues: 'Our artillery, with the exception of two 8-inch howitzers, was unequal to contend against theirs, many of which were 12-pounders. Our artillery endeavoured to shake them before the infantry advanced; but firing from the jungle I believe no officer could distinctly aim at any object, so that after a large consumption of ammunition the line advanced, with Sir Harry Smith's Division of two brigades in reserve. The men advanced well, considering the difficulties opposed to them. I led the left centre, and when we came opposite the Sikh batteries the fire was very heavy with grape and musketry. The infantry pressed on; and we gained that portion of the camp opposed to us, as did the right under Sir Hugh Gough. Sir J. Littler's brigades had inclined too much to their left, and the gap between his right and my left was considerable.

[1] Then the President of the Board of Control.

'In the meantime I was in the enemy's camp, from which we had driven them. Darkness was fast setting in. Mines and live shells were exploding and the tents and forage catching fire; that portion of the camp we had carried was in flames. It was impossible to proceed through the flames. We could not distinguish friend from foe, and we took up our ground as near to the edge of the burning camp as we could. On our right and left we heard incessant file-firing and discharges from the enemy's guns. In our front we had their burning camp, in our rear the jungle through which we had advanced.

'We had no alternative but to make the men lie down and be quiet. The Commander-in-Chief soon joined me. We knew nothing of what had passed on our flanks; and we agreed to keep the men together, to collect what troops we could, and if possible to communicate with Smith and Littler. The artillery was nowhere, but we considered it to be safe in our rear. In this state we lay on our arms, the enemy firing from his batteries, hurrahing, and firing mines during the night. The official details will report the conduct of the 80th Queen's, which I ordered at midnight to attack some guns, led by my aide-de-camp, Colonel Wood. These brave fellows had borne the brunt of the action during the attack; and now, though suffering from fatigue and excessive thirst, they patiently submitted to the cannonade, and obeyed the orders they received with celerity and courage. I had been on horseback since 4 the preceding morning, and I lay down successively with four of the British regiments, to ascertain their temper and give the encouragement required. I found myself again with my old Peninsular friends of the 29th, the 50th, the 31st, and the 9th, all in good heart.

'Towards the morning, the cries of the Sikhs and the tramp of bodies of men showed that they had reinforced that part of their position which we had not attacked. The fire of their guns still continued, as signals to that part of the army which had been worsted that their comrades still held their ground and required support, and everything announced that in the morning we should have a desperate struggle. The brave men in our line were re-formed. The Commander-in-Chief came to me and told me his opinion that we were in a critical and perilous state. I fully agreed, and we were both of one mind that we should attack the enemy's camp and carry it at all hazards.

'Having made every disposition for the morning's work, we waited impatiently for the break of day. Sir Hugh Gough led the right, and I the centre and left. I have in my official report related what passed, to which I refer you. The British infantry quite reminded me of the glorious days of the Peninsula. Depend upon it, the cheapest accession of force will be found to consist of British troops.

'At 11 o'clock a.m. [December 22nd] we were threatened by another attack. Camel-swivels came to our front and fired with some effect upon our infantry.

The enemy appeared behind the camels with a few thousand infantry and then made off. At 3 o'clock another demonstration was made of infantry, artillery, and cavalry. I threw a brigade of Littler's into the village of Firozsháh, where it was not only safe but could give protection to the horse artillery. The remainder of the infantry was in line, in a firm attitude to resist any attack. At this moment the British cavalry were suddenly seen to go off towards Firozpur, followed by the horse artillery. The infantry, with the greatest unconcern, held their ground and advanced when ordered. The enemy again retired, afraid of the infantry, which was actually abandoned by the cavalry and at least thirty pieces of artillery. We slept in the open air in rear of the infantry. The Sikhs were evidently in full retreat.

'The next morning [December 23rd] I rode into Firozpur to collect intelligence. I met the cavalry and artillery returning to the camp, and crowds of men who had either fled or lost their way. I also met the brigadier commanding, who stated that he had received an order from the acting Adjutant-General to save his cavalry and retire upon Firozpur. The other brigadier made a similar explanation. The horse artillery explained that, wanting ammunition, they had followed the cavalry. The officer who gave the order was Captain L——.'

I have given the above extracts from two separate letters, because, although they describe the same scenes, they vary in details and contain information hitherto unpublished.

Having myself ridden into Firozpur with the Governor-General on December 23rd, I was an eye-witness of his *rencontre* with the cavalry and artillery coming out of the town. The Governor-General was naturally very indignant when he approached the head of the column, and addressed them in unmeasured terms. He then turned to Captain L——, demanding an explanation from that unfortunate officer, who was evidently suffering from the effects of a sunstroke[1]. On being asked why he appeared in such a dress (having nothing on his legs but *paijamas*), he told us that during the action of the previous day his overalls had been so riddled with balls that they had dropped off! It was most unfortunate that his order was obeyed as coming from the Commander-in-Chief, who being on the right flank was totally ignorant of what was going on, while the camp was left more or less at the mercy of Tej Singh's force.

Good, however, sometimes comes out of evil. It has been surmised that the Sikhs, seeing this large force of cavalry moving to the left, imagined that their flank was being turned, and dreaded being cut off from the river. Others have thought that treachery on the part of Tej Singh was the true motive of his retreat. Certain it is that from want of ammunition our army was in a greater state of peril than even the night before. Happening to be alone with the Governor-

[1] He was shortly afterwards invalided home.

General at that moment—my brother being with Sir H. Gough—I can recollect the late Lord Delawarr, then Major West, riding up and delivering a message from the Commander-in-Chief. The men were lying down in the Sikh trenches, with only a few rounds left. The Governor-General exclaimed: 'Recollect, men, you must hold your ground to the last, and trust to your bayonets!' Our relief may be imagined when we saw the long line of Sikh infantry, camel-swivels, and artillery, moving slowly away towards the Sutlej.

Efforts were made, when the campaign was over, to ascertain the truth of these surmises, but no reliable evidence was forthcoming. The fact is on record that a fresh division of the Sikh army refused to attack a handful of British soldiers, defending the village they had captured early in the day, without ammunition and without the support of either artillery or cavalry. That some abandoned the army during the night is, I fear, painfully true. When the village was captured at break of day, and the Commander-in-Chief and the Governor-General passed down the line, the colours dropped and the men cheered. One officer commanding a Native regiment, whose men had only just turned up, stepped out and said: 'Sir, these cheers of my men are not worth having; only a few of the regiment were with me during the night.' Such occurrences were happily not common. It can only be remarked, in all fairness, that at Sobráon the Sepoys fought gallantly and kept up their old reputation for valour.

The official records soon gave to sorrowing friends the melancholy death-roll which throws a gloom over every victory. I can add but little to what Major W. Broadfoot has published with regard to his gallant brother. But I can say this, from personal knowledge, that no officer fell on the 21st who was more sincerely mourned by the Chief he had served so well. No one was held in more affectionate remembrance, and no one has ever better justified the high expectations which from the first were formed of his diplomatic and military abilities. It was my privilege to attend the gallant Somerset (Lord Raglan's son) in his last moments. A finer spirit was never called away from a short but active career. Munro and Hore, both aides-de-camp of the Governor-General and excellent officers, were also dead. The long list of wounded included Saunders Abbott; Lake, of the Engineers; Mills, who on that occasion took command of his old troop of Horse Artillery; and Becher, of the Quarter-Master-General's Department. These were all 'Politicals' except Becher, and had done good service in the Cis-Sutlej States. The remains of those that fell lie in the little church at Firozpur, but their memories live in the hearts of their comrades.

On the 24th of December, the Governor-General's camp was pitched at Firozpur. The *impedimenta* had arrived, and we at once settled down to our usual camp-life. The Commander-in-Chief remained with the main body near Firozsháh, until arrangements had been made for a forward movement. On

Christmas Day the Governor-General published a notification, which was read on every parade, congratulating the army on the complete success of their operations, and inviting them to assemble at headquarters to return thanks to Almighty God for His late mercies. When the 62nd Regiment joined the Commander-in-Chief's camp, a General Order was issued exculpating them from the reflections contained in Sir J. Littler's despatch, and making it known that they retired by the order of their Brigadier after extremely heavy loss, and that the despatch was never intended for publication.

The following extracts from a letter of Sir H. Hardinge to Lord Ripon on December 27th sum up the results:—'I have now closed my narrative. Our success with the defensive force has been complete. Every combination for repelling the enemy, which the suddenness of the attack required, has been successful. The celerity of the march, the rapid movement of the Ludhiána force of 5000 men on Basián, securing the supplies and adding the above numbers to the relieving force from Ambála, were dispositions as prudent as they were valuable for securing our success. The instructions to Littler to move from Firozpur and form his junction, in spite of the enemy attempting to prevent our progress with 60,000 men and 150 guns, prove the accuracy of the combinations. The battle of the 21st was fought with the greatest number that we could bring against the enemy. No delay could have augmented our force; it would only have augmented that of the enemy. The postponement of the battle was nearly impossible. Water was not to be had. All the difficulties of the approach to the Sikh camp would have been the same as they were on the 21st. Littler joined at one o'clock; and although time was lost, the want of daylight, while it rendered our decided success less secure, caused the enemy to abandon that portion of the position which had not been attacked, and was as detrimental to him as it was hazardous to us.

'I deplore the derangement of mind which caused the unfortunate order to be given to the cavalry. If advantage be taken of this grave error, it will lead to useful results. I know I am not responsible for military misconceptions, nor will I say one word on the extraordinary position in which I am placed. I have never desponded; and now I can sincerely assure you that, as far as the results of these difficult operations are concerned, I am perfectly satisfied. No impression has been made on the loyalty of the Sepoys. Victory has re-assured the wavering. Everything is in a state of security, which will be materially increased in four or five days, when the Meerut force arrives.'

I have been induced to insert copious extracts from the Governor-General's correspondence with the authorities at home and others, because such letters speak for themselves. The formal despatches, recording these eventful and sanguinary actions, necessarily omit much that should now be made known after the lapse of nearly fifty years. They were at the time merely the outline and framework of information, which up to the present period has for many reasons been kept in the background and not seen the light.

The news of the battles of Múdkí and Firozsháh aroused the greatest excitement in England, not unmixed with anxiety. The despatches arrived on February 7th, 1846, having been conveyed by an Austrian steamer to Trieste, on the breakdown of the mail steamer at Malta. The Tower guns were fired in celebration of the victory; but it was felt that serious conflicts were yet imminent, and that no one could foretell what might be the result. All that was known was that the Sikhs had been driven from two positions with the loss of their guns; and that the largest British force which had ever been mustered on the plains of India was still facing the enemy on the banks of the Sutlej. The general uneasiness in the public mind was shared by the Government, which resolved that certain contingencies must be provided for.

Lord Ripon, who, as President of the Board of Control, was the mouthpiece of communication between the Cabinet and the Governor-General, wrote to the latter in the following terms on February 24th:—

'The Cabinet have decided that it is indispensably necessary that some means should be taken whereby the command of all the operations in the field should be under you. It has a very strange and somewhat unseemly appearance that the Governor-General should be acting as second in command to the Commander-in-Chief in the field; and as these Punjab affairs are, and must necessarily be, so much mixed up with political matters, it is quite reasonable that the same head should direct both. We think that the best mode in which this could be done is by giving you (as was done in the case of Lord Wellesley in 1800) the commission of "Captain-General and Commander-in-Chief." This would place you in the position in which we wish to see you upon public and obvious grounds, and the commission would be so worded as not in any degree to point to any distrust of Gough. Lord Wellesley's commission was not given him when he first went out in 1797, but was given afterwards for special reasons assigned. The possession of the same powers will not *compel* you to exercise the power given you at all times and upon all occasions, but it will enable you at your own discretion to avail yourself of it.'

This letter was subsequently modified by another, dated March 7th:—

'We found so much difficulty and technical doubt as to the Letters Patent which I mentioned to you in my last letter of the 24th, and the law officers considered Lord Wellesley's case so inapplicable to yours, that we have been compelled to abandon the plan. We are, however, so convinced of the absolute necessity of meeting the difficulty of the case that we have adopted a course suggested by the Duke of Wellington, and explained in a Secret Committee Despatch of this day's date, that you should have a Letter of Service from the Queen to enable you as Lieutenant-General on the Staff to command personally the troops in India. The Duke has promised to write to the General, and to point out to him that this measure is one of absolute necessity under the very peculiar circumstances of a great crisis in India.'

The above extracts are now published for the first time. Few are even aware of their existence. But any biography of Lord Hardinge, however short, would not be accurate and complete without a record of this correspondence. So rapid, however, was the course of events that, before the second of these letters was written, not only had the crowning victory of Sobráon been won, but the British army had marched to Lahore without firing a shot after crossing the Sutlej. The necessity which had arisen no longer existed. None the less did the Governor-General appreciate the confidence in him which actuated the Cabinet in proposing that he should exercise supreme authority in matters military as well as political.

It remains only to observe that, up to the end of his administration, no friction occurred between the Governor-General and the Commander-in-Chief. The former had no reason to complain that his suggestions on military questions were disregarded; and the latter was glad to be supported by the advice of his colleague in every important crisis. The feeling of Sir H. Hardinge at the time may be learned from the following letter, which he addressed to the President of the Council at Calcutta on January 5th, 1846, only a fortnight after Firozsháh: 'I never can make any arrangement by which Sir Hugh Gough's supersession would lead to my appointment. The letters I annex will show the manner in which I am now compelled to interfere, and to take the whole of the military responsibility upon myself.' Four months afterwards (May 2nd), when the Letter of Service had reached him, he wrote again to the President of the Council in the same spirit: 'The other affair of appointing me a Lieutenant-General on the Staff is more embarrassing. But I have taken my line and done my best; and as the suspension of the order can do no harm, I hope equally to spare his [Gough's] feelings by preventing the publication of an arrangement made under very different circumstances from those in which we are now placed.'

CHAPTER VIII

ALÍWÁL AND SOBRÁON

To return to the operations of the army. The Commander-in-Chief had established his head-quarters at Sultán Khán Wála, and had made a personal reconnaissance of the banks of the Sutlej at Sobráon. On the 5th January, 1846, predatory bands of Sikhs advanced to Ludhiána, burning a few of the bungalows of the civil and military residents which had been evacuated. Brigadier Godby was in the Fort with three Native regiments, an adequate force for its defence. About the same time Ranjúr Singh, with a regular Sikh force of 8000 men and 70 guns, crossed the Sutlej a few miles from Ludhiána. Some have thought that his object was to intercept the siege train coming from Delhi; others, that he hoped to divide the British army. Sir Harry Smith with an ample force (the troops from Meerut having now come up) was despatched to the relief of Ludhiána. He soon discovered that Ranjúr Singh had broken up his camp on the river and marched to Badhowál, a village which rested on the Ludhiána road directly between that city and the relieving force. There were three roads leading to Ludhiána, within two, three, and five miles respectively of Badhowál. Sir Harry Smith chose the road along which the Ludhiána force was advancing to join him; upon which Ranjúr Singh, bending round one wing of his army, completely enveloped his flank. As Sir Harry Smith wrote in his despatch, 'The enemy thus outflanked me and my whole force. I therefore gradually withdrew my troops in échelon of battalions, the cavalry in échelon of squadrons, in the direction of Ludhiána, momentarily expecting to see the approach of the Ludhiána force. The line was thrown back, and the movements of the cavalry under Brigadier Cureton were the most perfect I ever saw.'

On the 19th, the Governor-General wrote to Sir Harry Smith to lose no time in marching on Ludhiána by Jagráon, where he was to pick up the 53rd Queen's. So anxious was he on this point, that in the middle of the night he rode down to the Commander-in-Chief's camp to request him to reinforce Smith at once. Wheeler's brigade was ordered to march for that purpose during the night, as no risk was too great to ensure an ample force for driving the Sikhs across the Sutlej.

The ensuing operations are thus commented upon by the Governor-General:—'Wheeler made a mistake by marching on the 22nd to Sidham instead of Jagráon. He first heard that Smith had attacked the Sikhs and beaten them on the 21st, and therefore took the direct road. This movement threatened the enemy's rear, who retired from Badhowál in a fright; so did Wheeler when he found him so close. On the 21st Smith, having been joined by H.M.'s 53rd, marched from Jagráon on Ludhiána, and chose to beard the Sikh army by passing close to the Fort at Badhowál where they had entrenched themselves. Godby's brigade, only six miles off, not being aware of Smith's march, although Smith had written to him, did not move out to his assistance, so that after a sharp cannonade Smith's baggage was completely cut off. Nothing makes people in India so angry as losing their comforts. "Disaster," "defeat," and every harsh word was used. I rode down to the Commander-in-Chief's camp early in the morning of the 27th; and after agreeing as to the great importance of the movement, we ordered Brigadier Taylor to move from Dharmkot to Jagráon, while an order was sent to Smith to attack. The next morning we heard the firing, and another order was sent to Smith to the same effect, which was conveyed to him by Major Lawrence, my Political Agent. On that morning Smith moved out, found the enemy—who had been reinforced by 4000 infantry and 12 guns—advancing against him, attacked and gained a brilliant victory.

'Gough was then so extremely anxious to storm the entrenched camp at Sobráon, with 80 or 90 guns and a force varying from 40,000 to 50,000 men, that I went back to camp rather than give way to his request. To cripple the British force without a reasonable prospect of capturing 60 or 70 guns would not be justifiable. I have never considered the Commander-in-Chief's position disadvantageous, for the enemy dare not venture out; and until our ammunition arrives, which it will on the 6th, it is impossible for them to undertake any important operation. To illustrate the dangers, I must observe that Smith at the close of the last action had no ammunition left.'

Ranjúr Singh is described by Sir Hugh Gough in his despatch as taking up an entrenched position at Badhowál, supporting himself on his fort. Threatened on either flank by Smith and Wheeler, he finally moved down to the Sutlej. Smith, being now reinforced by Wheeler, and having effected his junction with Godby's brigade from Ludhiána, marched out a distance of six miles to meet the enemy. The despatches recording the battle of Alíwál are matter of history: how after deploying into line Smith took ground to the right, and carrying the village of Alíwál, precipitated himself on the left and centre; how the enemy was driven back, while a squadron of the 16th Lancers under Major Smyth and Captain Pearson carried everything before them—charging through a Sikh square of infantry, a feat seldom accomplished even against Asiatic troops; how the 53rd carried the village at the point of the bayonet, while the Horse Artillery under Major Laurenson dashed among the flying infantry, committing the greatest havoc. The battle was won; every gun the enemy had fell into our hands, to the number of 52. All the Sikh forts were then blown up; and the force under Sir Harry Smith soon proceeded to join the Commander-in-Chief before Sobráon.

The battle of Alíwál had the effect of damping the

ardour of the Sikh troops. They rallied, however, in a way that bore evidence of their undaunted pluck. The remnant soon helped to swell the numbers of the main body, now massed at Sobráon. Cureton's cavalry brigade in the two days' action had covered the movements of Smith's Division in a manner which proved how that arm can be effectually utilised when well handled. It was maintained by some that their skilful manœuvring had in reality saved Smith's force from defeat. Suffice it to say, that this action contributed in no small degree to the total overthrow of the Khálsa army on the 10th February at the memorable battle of Sobráon.

As soon as the news of the victory of Alíwál reached head-quarters a gala parade of the whole force was ordered. The troops had recovered from the fatigues and privations of their preliminary operations, and now looked fit to go anywhere. There were the 31st, the 29th, the 50th, the 9th, the 80th, with the 9th Lancers and the 3rd Light Dragoons, who had infused such terror into the Sikh ranks on the night of the 21st December, and other regiments with many glorious names on their colours. As the two Chiefs rode down the line to announce the recent victory, they were greeted by cheers such as Englishmen alone can give. It was well known that a week would probably bring with it another sanguinary contest; and the thought must have crossed most minds that another such action as that of the 21st December would plunge many a distant home in mourning.

Major Henry Lawrence had by this time arrived at the Governor-General's head-quarters, to succeed Major Broadfoot as Political Agent. I can see him now in his long 'chogah,' with his Van Dyck beard and lathy figure. We little thought that he was destined subsequently to play so important a part in the history of India. The Governor-General had also fixed his eye on John Lawrence; and on these two brothers the future destinies of the Punjab in a great measure rested. Many were the pleasant rides we had from Firozpur to Sobráon two or three times a week. Starting at daybreak in the fresh air of the morning, we were then a group of joyous spirits, the Governor-General heading the cavalcade on his favourite Arab Miáni, and followed by the escort of the body-guard.

In the camp at Sobráon there was naturally disappointment at the slow progress of the siege train. 'The army,' says Herbert Edwardes [1], in the *Calcutta Review*, was 'sickening for want of a battle; a malignant fever or epidemic horrors must have broken out at Sobráon had it been delayed another week.' The first portion of the siege train, with reserve ammunition for 100 guns, reached the camp on the 7th and 8th February. On the 8th Sir Henry Smith's Division, which had been detached for the Ludhiána operations, rejoined the Commander-in-Chief. On the 10th was fought the battle of Sobráon.

Meanwhile, the days passed in constant recon-

[1] He was at this time aide-de-camp to Sir Hugh Gough.

noitring and outpost duty. There was an advanced post at Rhodawála, where the staff kept a continual look-out. By a sort of mutual understanding between the contending armies, the British evacuated this post at nightfall, to be again occupied by them when the day broke; and this exchange of duties was scrupulously observed without opposition. Between this outpost and the entrenched camp of the enemy stretched a tract of low jungle; and it was one of the events of the day to watch General Gilbert, a noted pig-sticker, riding after the boars, which took him pretty close to the enemy's range, and although this repeatedly happened we never heard of his being molested.

A few days before the battle, Sir Henry Hardinge met with a severe fall while returning to his camp. His horse, an Arab which had just arrived from Bombay, came down, bruising his leg very severely. This did not prevent him from carrying on his heavy duties and correspondence as usual; and when the tidings of the approach of the siege train reached him, he hurried to the Commander-in-Chief's camp in a light mule carriage.

I must now glance at the conferences which took place between the two Chiefs before the attack commenced. They agreed that it would be highly imprudent to assault the entrenched position until it had been shaken by the fire of twenty heavy howitzers and mortars. The Governor-General addressed the Commander-in-Chief on the 7th February and then joined him at head-quarters. He saw Colonel Brooke of the Artillery and Captain Baker of the Engineers, who agreed as to the feasibility of an assault after a heavy cannonade. Colonel Benson was sent to report this to the Commander-in-Chief, who entirely concurred in the proposal. The next day Brigadier Smith, of the Engineers, came to the Governor-General and threw doubts on the plan of the attack. He was then sent with Colonel Benson to the Commander-in-Chief, who expressed his regret at the vacillation displayed by the engineer and artillery officers. They were all assembled at head-quarters the next morning, and their opinions were still unfavourable. Sir H. Gough reported this by letter, leaving the decision to the Governor-General. On returning to Firozpur, Sir Henry Hardinge consulted Major Abbott of the Engineers and Major Lawrence the Political Agent, who was also a field-officer of artillery. They both agreed that an attack as proposed was practicable. In his next letter he authorised the Commander-in-Chief to attempt it, concluding with these words: 'If, upon the fullest consideration, the artillery can be brought into play, I recommend you to attack; if it cannot, and you anticipate a heavy loss, I would recommend you not to attempt it.' The next morning the artillery and engineer officers were again assembled; and when the Governor-General's letter containing Major Abbott's opinion was read to them, they changed their views and sanctioned the attack as proposed. The Commander-in-Chief then reported to the Governor-General that the engineer and artillery officers had concurred in its practicability; that his suggestions were excellent and should be carried out. It was agreed that the right flank should be cannonaded, and the Sikh camp swept from right to left.

The above account is condensed from a private letter of the Governor-General to Lord Ripon, dated Lahore, 16th February. It will be seen that the two Chiefs were perfectly agreed. The result will show how difficult it is in war to carry out with certainty any scheme, however well considered beforehand.

The Commander-in-Chief, in his despatch reporting the details of the battle, states that there had devolved upon him the arduous task of attacking a position covered with formidable entrenchments, and occupied by not fewer than 30,000 men with seventy pieces of artillery, united by a good bridge to a reserve on the opposite bank of the river.

It was intended that the siege batteries and disposable field artillery should be put in position on an extended semicircle, embracing within its fire the works of the Sikhs. This was carried out. A heavy mist hung over the plain as the day began to dawn. When it broke, the Governor-General mounted his horse, although still suffering from his fall, and then for two hours the plain reverberated with the incessant roar of heavy guns. The Commander-in-Chief came to the Governor-General and stated his fears that the artillery had produced very little effect.

It was decided, however, that the attack should proceed. On the right, Sir R. Dick's leading brigade advanced with great steadiness and carried the entrenchments. I was close to the Governor-General at that moment, when we saw our second line giving way; but it soon re-formed outside the breastwork and again advanced. The Governor-General writes: 'The moment was critical, and I ordered General Gilbert's Division, which was a mile to the right, to move forward. The Commander-in-Chief had given a similar order on the right flank.'

Gilbert's movement had been originally intended only as a feint; but the check which the second line had met with made it absolutely necessary that the feint should be turned into a real attack. Being now face to face with the strongest part of the Sikh entrenchments, the line, which had hitherto advanced with great steadiness, suddenly began to waver under the murderous fire of grape and canister. 'Rally those men,' the Governor-General shouted. No sooner were the words out of his mouth than Colonel Wood, his aide-de-camp, galloped to the centre of the line, and seizing the colours from the hands of the ensign carried them to the front. In a moment they had rallied and stormed the breastworks simultaneously with the brigades of Dick's Division, who, having experienced a similar check, had also recovered their lost ground and were now engaged in what may be called a hand-to-hand encounter with the Sikh infantry.

It should be observed that these regiments carried the works with the bayonet alone, and without firing a shot. On the right the same results had followed the assault of Sir Harry Smith's Division. They too, for a second, had winced under a hailstorm of bullets, which it seemed impossible to weather. At this crisis the cavalry were ordered up under Sir Joseph Thackwell, who rode with his squadrons in single file through an opening in the entrenchment. It seemed as if they were doomed to destruction. Many fell in the ranks when within the camp. But the 3rd Light Dragoons, showing the same invincible bravery as on the night of the 21st of December, quickly re-formed and charged the serried ranks of the Sikh infantry.

Never perhaps was so obstinate a contest carried on to the end; never before was such cohesion displayed in the ranks of the Khálsa army. Compelled to retire, they gave way in such admirable order as to excite the admiration of the British soldiers. At last the fire slackened, and then ensued a scene which defies description. Pressed on all sides by our advancing infantry, the enemy were hemmed in in one confused mass at the head of the bridge, there to be shot down or hurled into the river below. Happening to be an eye-witness of what then occurred, I saw the bridge at that moment overcrowded with guns, horses, and soldiers of all arms, swaying to and fro, till at last with a crash it disappeared in the running waters, carrying with it those who had vainly hoped to reach the opposite shore. The river seemed alive with a struggling mass of men. The artillery, now brought down to the water's edge, completed the slaughter. Few escaped; none, it may be said, surrendered. The Sikhs met their fate with that resignation which distinguishes their race.

It may be asked why such indiscriminate destruction was dealt out to so gallant a foe. The men's passions were roused. They were not forgetful of the treatment their officers and comrades had met with from the Khálsa army. The battlefield of Firozsháh disclosed horrible mutilations amongst the British officers and men who had fallen into the enemy's hands. The men vowed vengeance, and inflicted it. Moreover, had not the Khálsa army been annihilated at Sobráon, they would have rallied again and protracted a contest north of the river, which it was desirable on the grounds of humanity should, if possible, be brought to a close.

Passing through the Sikh camp on our return we saw Sir R. Dick, a Peninsular veteran, lying on the ground mortally wounded; a little further on Havelock (of Lucknow) was standing over his favourite Arab, which had just been shot under him; Brigadier Taylor, too, had fallen, and others whose services could ill be spared. The total number of killed amounted to 320, of wounded to 2063. The lowest estimate of the Sikh loss is 8000. The trophies of the victory comprised 67 pieces of artillery and 200 camel-swivels. Prince Waldemar and his aides-de-camp were again present in the field. As true soldiers, they were not satisfied with being distant spectators, but were continually under fire.

And here I would remark that, as the truth was not concealed in the earlier part of this narrative with regard to the Native troops firing into the air at Múdkí, so should the facts be now told concerning their conduct in the closing action of the campaign. I can personally vouch for the opinion then expressed by the Governor-General, and repeated on many subsequent occasions. He was more than surprised at seeing with his own eyes the steady support the Native regiments afforded their European comrades. The advance of Gilbert's and Dick's Divisions was perfect; and if for a moment there was wavering, it was shared equally by the Queen's regiments. It was, however, momentary, and both forces carried the works at the point of the bayonet. The Ghúrka battalions behaved admirably, and the returns in the Native regiments prove by the losses recorded how well they fought.

Let me now give one or two extracts from the Governor-General's correspondence, dated from Simla in the following April :—'I should have preferred more troops in support of the attacking force, as explained in my previous letter, because the assistance, whenever it might require to be given, would have been given by the rear taking the enemy in reverse; whereas by having it in front of his batteries, when the attacking force required support, we could only give it by the front taking the enemy's batteries by assault. Thus, when the attacking column was repulsed, I was obliged to order Gilbert forward at once, who after a gallant advance was for the moment driven back; but the attacking column having been thus relieved, in its turn rushed forward, and from that moment had no check. In like manner Smith's Division had to carry very strong batteries. The leading brigade was repulsed; the brigade in reserve carried the works. Thus the three Divisions engaged were each in their turn checked, rallied, and carried everything before them. As regards the military view of our recent operations, there can be no doubt that, if the enemy had avoided a general action and had retired with its army to Lahore, Govindgarh, and Amritsar, our operations at this advanced season, with three sieges in hand, must have been carried on at great disadvantage, as shown by the unanimous opinion of the engineer and artillery officers. The exploit of the army is one of the most daring in the annals of our military history. The guns captured were sixty-seven. On the evening of the battle six regiments near Firozpur crossed into the enemy's territory, and on the 16th the whole army, with the exception of three brigades, was concentrated at Kasúr. We have now taken in battle 220 pieces of artillery, of which 80 pieces exceed in calibre anything known in European warfare. The weight of the Sikh gun in proportion to its calibre is much heavier than ours, and the range of the six-pounder is longer.

The recoil on the carriage is less, and their guns do not heat so rapidly as ours in firing.'

At 1 p.m. the battle of Sobráon was over. At 1.30 Colonel Wood, hardly recovered from his wound, was riding off to Sir J. Grey's Division at Haruku to order him to prepare for crossing the river immediately; he then rode on to Firozpur, twenty-five miles from head-quarters, to deliver the same order, and at 5 p.m. returned half-way to meet the Governor-General. On the 13th February, the whole army had crossed, with the exception of three brigades. On the 12th, the Governor-General himself with his staff crossed the bridge of boats. Abbott and Napier[1] both superintended the operation. We witnessed regiment after regiment crossing the bridge. The men stepped out as if conscious of the victory in which they had participated. Three general actions had told their tale; some corps were lamentably weak, but flushed with victory they were ready for anything.

[1] Lord Napier of Magdala.

CHAPTER IX

The Treaty of Lahore

March, 1846

The army marched that same day to Kasúr, within thirty-two miles of Lahore, with no appearance of any hostile force in its front. Having been joined by six Native regiments and 100 European recruits on the road, it was now almost as strong numerically as before the action. The following extract from a letter from Kasúr, dated February, 1846, shows that at that early period the Governor-General had already sketched out his Punjab policy for the Home authorities:—'A diminution of the strength of such a warlike nation on our weakest frontier seems to me to be imperatively required. I have, therefore, determined to take a strong and fertile district between the Sutlej and the Beas. This will cover Ludhiána and bring us within a few miles of Amritsar, with our back to the Hills. In a military sense, it will be very important—it will weaken the Sikhs and punish them in the eyes of Asia. I shall demand one million and a half in money as compensation; and if I can arrange to make Ghuláb Singh and the Hill tribes independent, including Kashmír, I shall have weakened this warlike republic. Its army must be disbanded and reorganised. The numbers of the artillery must be limited. The Mahárájá must himself present the keys of Govindgarh and Lahore, where the terms must be dictated and signed.'

In the main this policy was carried through. The Lahore Darbár had hoped that the Governor-General would have proposed a Resident with a Subsidiary Force—a system against which he had constantly entered his protest, and which would have inevitably led to insurrection, only to be put down by British bayonets. The other alternative was annexation. The extension of the British Empire to the Indus, however captivating to a certain school of politicians, was at that time impossible on military grounds. The absolute necessity of waiting for ammunition for 100 siege-guns until the army could advance, and the equally strong necessity of a siege train such as would deter the Sikh Darbár from making the war a war of sieges, were paramount considerations in which Sir Charles Napier (who had now joined the army) entirely concurred. The intermediate course which the Governor-General proposed of re-establishing a Sikh government, balanced against the Muhammadan population and greatly weakened for hostile aggression, offered, in his eyes, the best solution of a very difficult problem.

On the 18th of February, when the Governor-General's camp had been pitched within a short distance of Lahore, there arrived a deputation of the Sikh Sardárs, headed by Ghuláb Singh, who nominally held the post of Minister. He brought with him not only the usual number of attendants, elephants, presents, &c., but also the little Mahárájá himself—a charming child of eight years—'acting his part,' as the Governor-General describes him, 'without any fear and with all the good breeding peculiar to the Eastern people.' The Minister, having in the Mahárájá's presence acceded to the preliminary conditions of the British proposals, presented his tokens of allegiance, and retired to confer with Mr. Currie and Major Lawrence on the details of the Treaty. The Mahárájá remained in the Governor-General's camp, and accompanied him on his march to Lahore. On the same day a proclamation was issued promising protection, on the part of the British Government, to all persons at Lahore and elsewhere who peaceably continued in their usual employments of trade and industry.

On the 20th of February every arrangement had been made, and Mr. Currie proceeded to the Mahárájá's camp to conduct him to his palace in the citadel. He was attended by the civil and military staff, and accompanied by an escort of four cavalry regiments and artillery under Brigadier Cureton. About a mile from the camp he was met by Ghuláb Singh and the principal Sikh Sardárs. Salutes were fired, and a procession formed which made the circuit of the city until it reached the palace, where Mr. Currie took his leave. Two days afterwards the Governor-General issued a General Order, thanking the army for the important services they had rendered, and enjoining the strictest discipline during their occupation of the city. On this occasion a gratuity of twelve months' batta was announced as a reward for the services of the army of the Sutlej.

On the 8th of March the Ministers and Sardárs assembled in Major Lawrence's tent to sign the Treaty. The letter of the Mahárájá, expressing gratitude to the Governor-General, was read in their presence; but at the close of that letter a new request was added, that a British force should be left at Lahore for a limited period. It was represented, on the part of the Governor-General, that the reasons for this new proposal should be stated in writing; and on this promise being given, the Treaty was signed and the meeting broke up. The promised explanation was then sent. It stated that it was the 'earnest and sincere desire of the Darbár that British troops with intelligent officers should, for some months, as circumstances seemed to require, be left at Lahore for the protection of the Mahárájá and his Government.' On the 9th it was announced in a General Order that the Treaty would be ratified on that day. It contained an additional clause to the effect that, at the earnest solicitation of the Mahárájá, the Governor-General had consented to occupy the town and citadel of Lahore with British troops for a limited period, in order that opportunity might be afforded to the Sikh Darbár to reorganise its army according to the stipulations of the Treaty.

The Governor-General had, no doubt, some misgivings before he consented to this occupation. Hosts of critics and advisers prophesied a repetition of the Kábul disaster; even Sir Charles Napier thought it involved great risk, and on that ground volunteered to command the garrison. The Governor-General stated in reply that, however much he valued his eminent services, he felt, in consideration of Sir Charles's health, it would not be fair to him that such an offer should be accepted.

On the same day (March 9th) the Darbár was held in the state tent at 4 p.m. It was attended by the Governor-General, the Commander-in-Chief, the Governor of Sind (Sir Charles Napier), and the principal European and native officers of the army. The Mahárájá, accompanied by Lál Singh, Ghuláb Singh, Tej Singh, and thirty Sardárs, took his seat in a chair of state which had been prepared for him opposite the Governor-General, who was supported on his right and left by the chief civil and military officers. The scene was a striking one. The little prince, loaded with Oriental jewellery and with the Sikh aigrette in his turban, looked on with perfect calmness. Whether his intelligence could grasp the peculiarity of his position could not be fathomed; but when the Governor-General rose to address the chiefs his dark eyes became animated, and were fixed on the Lord Sahib dictating terms to the descendant of the great Ranjít.

In his address the Governor-General dwelt on the fact that the Government had in no way provoked the war, and that the proof of its sincerity was to be found in the moderation of its proposals. With reference to the occupation of Lahore by British troops, he announced that he could in no case consent that the troops should remain longer than the end of the year, and concluded his speech in these words:—'Success or failure is in your own hands; my co-operation shall not be wanting; but if you neglect this opportunity, no aid on the part of the British Government can save the State.'

The Sikh chiefs expressed their gratitude, and their resolution to follow the advice of the Governor-General. Then followed a pause, for the Governor-General had whispered to the Foreign Secretary that the Koh-i-núr was by the terms of the Treaty to be delivered to the Queen of England, and that the famous gem, 'The Mountain of Light,' should be submitted for their inspection. His wish was at once communicated to the Sikh Ministers. Another pause, and more whispers. At last, a small tin box enveloped in a shabby cloth was brought in, containing the diamond which is now worn by the Empress of India on state occasions. Many have since seen it; to us it appeared to be wanting in that brilliancy which is the charm of smaller stones. W. Edwards, Under-Secretary in the Foreign Department, was manifestly uncomfortable; for to him had been confided the precious stone which was now going the round of the assembled dignitaries. But when it was restored to his keeping, he resumed his equanimity. Mr. Bosworth

Smith's *Life of Lord Lawrence* relates how the Koh-i-núr was afterwards delivered to John Lawrence for safe custody, and how Lawrence for a time lost the priceless gem!

Those who were acquainted with Lahore in those days can alone form an idea of its picturesque aspect. Surrounded by the ruined tombs of the Muhammadan kings, the city with its fortifications, its colossal pillars and minarets, presented an appearance which made it rank among the most striking of our Eastern towns, Amritsar alone excepted. It is now bereft to a great extent of its old attractions. Cantonments with their barracks and bungalows, however indicative of the security of civilisation, do not charm the eye. The procession of the Mahárájá in his circuit round the city was unique in effect. The colours of the dresses, the line of elephants, contrasting with the display of troops, were a sight not easily to be effaced from our recollection.

I had a delicate business to carry out at this time on my own private account. It was purely artistic, and I had little hope of being successful. It had been intimated to me that Lál Singh had no objection to sit for his portrait, although he was at the time hourly engaged in conferences and negotiations. However, whilst I was waiting by appointment in the court-yard of the palace, a 'pardah' was drawn aside suddenly, and Lál Singh rode in equipped in a complete suit of armour. I longed at the moment for the touch of a Velasquez; the subject would have been worthy of him. For the Rání's favourite was every inch a Sikh, as remarkable for his personal appearance as he was infamous for his cruelty and excesses.

Before leaving Lahore, the Governor-General, accompanied by Sir Hugh Gough and Sir Charles Napier, reviewed the army of the Sutlej. On that occasion were drawn up the regiments which had fought many years before in the Peninsula, in company with the three distinguished soldiers who now went down the line. Crippled by the losses they had sustained in four general actions, they were still a proud remnant of that force which in the previous year had been massed on the frontier. The 31st, which before the campaign had mustered 850 bayonets, marched past with less than half its original strength. The 9th, with a strength of 874 before Múdkí, could only bring up 450. The gallant 50th, the 'dirty half-hundred,' had lost 300 men killed and wounded; and other regiments had suffered in proportion. It was an imposing sight, but not devoid of sad recollections. As the Governor-General passed along, there was a word for each regiment. When he halted before Sir C. Napier's old corps he told them how that distinguished general had fought with them in the Peninsula, and how proud he was of their behaviour in the late battles. It was too much for the gallant Napier. In vain he tried to speak. He could only wave his hand as an acknowledgment.

Sir Charles's dress was not strictly according to

regulation—a pith helmet, a native leather jacket, breeches and long boots made up his 'kit.' This dress he had never changed since his arrival in camp. Had the war been protracted, the contingent of 12,000 men which he had brought up from Sind would have swelled our strength; and no man was more depressed when he failed to reach the army in time. But he quite concurred with the Governor-General that annexation at that time was impossible. In this he must have been sincere: for a protracted war would undoubtedly have brought him to the front, and his political antecedents certainly pointed to his approval of the principle of extending our frontier. Ever kind-hearted, with a determined spirit and great professional ability, he left us prepossessed with the conviction that he was no ordinary man, however much his opponents may have declaimed against him—perhaps not without some excuse.

To return, however, to the Treaty. Its principal provisions were the abandonment by the Sikh Darbár of the strip of territory between the Beas and the Sutlej; the payment of a million and a half sterling as indemnity for the expenses of the war—should the Darbár be unable to pay the whole of this sum, or to give satisfactory security, the provinces of Kashmír and Házára were to be ceded as an equivalent—fifty lakhs of rupees (£500,000) were to be paid on or before the ratification of the Treaty; the Sikh army was restricted to twenty-five battalions of infantry and 12,000 cavalry; and all the guns pointed against the British troops were to be surrendered. By Article 12 the Mahárájá agreed to recognise the independent sovereignty of Ghuláb Singh in such territories as might be assigned to him. The occupation of the city by British troops till the end of the year had already been agreed upon. Lál Singh, Bhai Rám Singh, Tej Singh, Diwán Dena Náth were the signatories of this historic document. The Treaty concluded at the same time by the British Government with Ghuláb Singh made over to him all the territory eastward of the Indus and westward of the Rávi River, on the payment of seventy-five lakhs of rupees (£750,000). The limits of these territories were not to be changed without the consent of the British Government.

Such was the Treaty of Lahore. It added to the Company's dominions territory yielding a revenue of £400,000, and strengthened our right flank so as to protect Simla, Ludhiána, and Ambála. Some have blamed the Government for the transfer of Kashmír to Ghuláb Singh; but such critics have probably not calculated the number of men necessary to hold that province, or the probable revenue which would have been derived from its annexation. Those, too, who cavil against Lord Hardinge's non-annexation policy, and who think, as Sir C. Napier did, that 'no Indian prince should exist,' must put to themselves this question: Could the Governor-General, with the military means at his disposal, have achieved such a conquest after Sobráon? There was at that time a deficit in the Indian treasury. The hot season was setting in, while four general actions had palpably weakened the strength of our European regiments. Must it not then occur to every one that in the event of insurrection, such as occurred not long after at Múltán, the presence of the British troops at Lahore, backed by the concentrated force under the Commander-in-Chief, would greatly facilitate the annexation of the whole province whenever such an extremity might become necessary?

With regard to the transfer of Kashmír to Ghuláb Singh, the Governor-General gives the following reasons in a letter written to a near relative:—'It was necessary last March to weaken the Sikhs by depriving them of Kashmír. The distance from Kashmír to the Sutlej is 300 miles of very difficult mountainous country, quite impracticable for six months. To keep a British force 300 miles from any possibility of support would have been an undertaking that merited a strait-waistcoat and not a peerage.' The arrangement made was the only alternative. The Government took away with one hand and gave with the other, as the exigencies of the case required; and as regards the honesty of the transaction, the names of Currie and Lawrence are a sufficient guarantee. Ghuláb Singh's character was not without reproach; but where was the native chief or minister to be found without similar blots on his escutcheon?

The most complete explanation of Lord Hardinge's views on this subject is to be found in a letter to

Lord Ellenborough, who had questioned the policy of rewarding what he termed Ghuláb Singh's treachery to the Lahore state. As criticisms similar to those of Lord Ellenborough have been prevalent, I think it right to quote passages from this letter at some length:—

'Ghuláb Singh was never Minister at Lahore for the administration of its affairs. Early in 1845 Jowahir Singh persuaded the army to march against Jamú. Ghuláb Singh, despairing of being able to defend himself, threw himself into the hands of the Pancháyats and was brought a prisoner to Lahore. He was there treated with great severity; and subsequently, when the army offered him the Wazírship, he repeatedly declined the offer. When the invasion took place, he remained at Jamú and took no part against us, but tendered his allegiance on condition of being confirmed in the possession of his own territories. This was neither conceded nor refused, as the paramount power did not think it becoming, while the armies were in presence of each other, to show any doubt as to the result by granting terms. I merely referred him to the terms of the Proclamation of December, when the Sikhs crossed the Sutlej. Nevertheless, it was clearly to be understood by the terms of that Proclamation that, if Ghuláb Singh took no part against us, he was entitled to consideration whenever the affairs of the Punjab came to be settled. It was evident that he had no cause of gratitude or attachment to the Lahore Darbár, by whose orders and intrigues his own family had been nearly exterminated, his possessions taken, and his son slain. During the whole of the campaign he had purposely kept aloof; not a single Hill soldier had fired a shot against us, so that the Government had every right to treat with him. They had their own interests, also, to attend to; which in policy required that the Sikh state should be weakened and that the Hills should be separated from the plains.

'Were we to be deterred from doing what was right, and what had been previously determined upon, because the Lahore Darbár, knowing he had not participated in their crimes, chose to employ him for a particular object as being the man most acceptable to us? Was he the Minister, and were not four other Commissioners associated with him for settling the terms of peace? After Múdkí and Firozsháh the Rání had implored him to come to Lahore and bring his troops to her aid. He sent evasive answers. After the battle of Alíwál more pressing invitations were sent, as he alone, in their opinion, could settle affairs with the English, because he had not taken part against them. He came to Lahore, protesting publicly in Darbár against all that had been done. He accepted the responsibility of attempting a settlement, but required the Rání to sign a paper that she would accede to the terms which he and the other four Commissioners should agree upon. He had been told by Major Lawrence on the 3rd of February, in a written document, that we appreciated his wisdom in not having taken up arms against us, and that his interests would be taken into consideration. The words of the Proclamation, dated 14th of February, were these: "The extent of the territory which it may be advisable to take will be determined by the conduct of the Darbár and by considerations for the security of the British frontier."

'These words were meant to include any arrangements which would render the Hills independent of the plains, which arrangement had been well considered before the battle of Sobráon. It was always intended that Ghuláb Singh, whose troops had not fired a shot, should have his case and position fully considered. What act of treason, then, had he committed against the Lahore state? He had done good service to us, which we had recognised before he was a Sikh Commissioner. After the war commenced, were we to abandon our policy and to treat the only man who had not lifted up his arm against us with indifference, because he came to head-quarters specially deputed by the Lahore Darbár to confer with us as one who had not joined in their unprovoked invasion? His forbearance was rewarded, because this forbearance was in accordance with an intended policy, and because the charge of treachery could not be substantiated.'

CHAPTER X

Kashmír and the Second Treaty of Lahore

December, 1846

The Governor-General now retired to Simla, to enjoy a few months' repose during the hot season. There I joined him later in the year, having first made an excursion into Kashmír. As Kashmír was in those days unknown to Englishmen, and as it figures somewhat prominently in the history of the time, I may perhaps be pardoned for introducing here some personal reminiscences. The party included Lord Elphinstone (afterwards Governor of Bombay), Captain Nicholson (the hero of Delhi), my brother Captain A. Hardinge, with Dr. Walker and Major Bates. Needless to say that we possessed no diplomatic powers; but we kept our eyes open, and reported all that we observed.

On our way to Kashmír, we visited Ghuláb Singh in his hill-fortress of Jamú. Nothing could exceed the cordiality of the reception we met with, all being done of course with a special object. When we were summoned to Ghuláb's presence, a diplomatic difficulty arose. Nicholson, so distinguished in after years, was our interpreter and master of the ceremonies, and he insisted on our taking off our boots before our introduction to the Rájá. Being in full uniform, we held a consultation with Lord Elphinstone, and unanimously agreed that we would not make fools of ourselves, merely to please a man who owed everything to the British. Imagine our surprise on seeing Nicholson enter, also in full uniform, with a pair of very baggy stockings on his feet! All I can say is, that while he was with us he never heard the last of it.

Our interview with the Rájá, a fine handsome old man with a long beard, was extremely interesting. He gave us a history of all his campaigns, and produced a sort of panorama painted by a native artist, portraying the events of his life. In one there was a group of men pouring what was evidently molten lead down a prisoner's throat. We asked what they were doing, upon which he laughed heartily, and pointing to the caldron said, 'They are making tea!' When we alluded to Kot Kángra holding out, he simply observed that Lál Singh was at the bottom of it all, and ought to be hanged; but he was sorry, at the same time, to speak thus of an old friend. He mentioned, too, the narrow escape he had had when the English garrison first occupied Lahore. According to his account, on returning one day from Lawrence's tent, he went to a shrine in the city to perform his devotions, and on rising to mount his horse the Fakír observed, 'It is not time yet.' He then waited about a quarter of an hour and again proposed to go. The Fakír again stopped him; but when half an hour had elapsed, he was allowed to go. He afterwards found out that a party of men hired by Lál Singh had been told off to murder him; and that these men, finding that he did not arrive at his house at the usual time, concluded he had gone round by some other street.

The next day we were off to Kashmír, but before starting we found that our shooting jackets had been taken away by the Court tailor. After some delay they were restored to us, not in their original tweed mixture but entirely covered with gold 'kin-kob.' Mounting our hill ponies among the salaams of the assembled multitude, we presented rather a strange aspect. None laughed more over it than our charming friend Lord Elphinstone, who headed the cavalcade.

From Jamú our route to the pass into the Kashmír valley was almost impracticable. We repeatedly had to dismount from our ponies and lead them along ledges of granite rock, descending abruptly into the 'khăd' below. Ghuláb Singh had given me his best pony—a perfect specimen of the hill breed, with a white mane reaching to the ground. We had not gone far before we heard shouting in our front. The unfortunate animal had lost its footing; and in spite of the efforts of the coolies to hold it until further assistance arrived, it was precipitated many thousand feet into the torrent below. Nor was this our only disaster. Two days' march further on I had stopped to sketch, sending on my tents and baggage to our halting-ground. Darkness overtook us through a miscalculation of time. It was dangerous to mount, so that it became necessary for us to crawl on our hands and feet whenever we reached an awkward spot in the narrow road. In one of these we came to a pool of water with a torrent running over the road. There was nothing for it but to drive the pony through the pool, hoping that he would reach the ground beyond in safety. To our horror, he too slipped; heavy thuds at intervals told us he had gone over. We waded through this pool, torches were sent out for us, and at last we reached the village. To our surprise the next morning we found the poor animal alive, with his fore and hind feet across a large fir-tree, and a water-fall pouring over him. He was rescued, but, strange to relate, was killed on our return journey by a similar accident.

The Governor of Kashmír at this time was the Shaikh Imám-ud-dín, who, in October of this very year, refused to recognise Ghuláb Singh's title under the Treaty of Lahore and brought upon himself a British expedition. Though we were received by the Shaikh with every mark of respect and honour, one circumstance caused us to suspect that appearances were deceptive. On our expressing a wish to visit the fort, in order to get a view of the far-famed lake, it was intimated to us that troops of the Sikh Darbár still held it, but that if we were inclined to go without any armed attendants we were at liberty to do so. To this we assented. We found none of Ghuláb Singh's troops in the fort, though they arrived shortly afterwards. Apart from this, we had nothing to complain of. Shooting parties were organised for us, and everything was done by the Shaikh to render our stay as pleasant as possible.

Here our party separated. I proceeded to join the Governor-General at Simla, accompanied only by our surgeon, Dr. Walker. On our way we had to pass Kot Kángra, and there heard for the first time of the surrender of the Sikh garrison. Kángra is so well described in the *Life of Lord Lawrence* by Mr. Bosworth Smith that I can add nothing to his picture. Imagine Edinburgh Castle, on a rock much more precipitous, encircled by a rushing torrent and completely commanded from the hills above, and you can form an idea of that Eastern Gibraltar. Without siege guns the place was impregnable. The Sikh garrison had refused to surrender, and simply laughed at us, till Wheeler and John Lawrence, who was then at the head of affairs in the Jálandhar Doáb, brought up the elephant battery. Roads were immediately cut in the rock: and these sagacious animals, when they were in single file, actually pushed up with their foreheads the ammunition waggons immediately in their front. Not a shot was fired. The white flag was immediately hoisted on the citadel, and the garrison laid down their arms.

Let us now follow the Governor-General to his retreat at Simla. The small bungalow overlooking the snowy range was modest enough compared with the Government House which has since been erected. I can see him now, pacing up and down the verandah, as he discussed with energy the contents of the latest 'dák' from Lahore with some of the secretariat. After the labours and excitement of the campaign, the repose now permitted and the pleasant reflection that his rule was nearly at an end were meat and drink to him.

Shortly after my arrival the mail-bags from England were opened, containing the list of honours for the army of the Sutlej. Few soldiers had better merited their rewards, which were distributed with no sparing hand. The two Chiefs received peerages, and Parliament voted to each an annuity of £3000 to sustain the dignity. It happened, however, that before the Cabinet could move in the matter, the Court of Directors had, by a unanimous vote, granted to Lord Hardinge a pension of £5000, charged on the revenues of India. It was obvious that no servant of the Crown could accept this double acknowledgment of his services; and Lord Hardinge was the last person to avail himself of such excessive liberality. In his absence, it fell to the lot of his wife to remove the difficulty which had arisen. In a letter from her, which was read in the House of Lords by Lord Lansdowne, she anticipated the expression of her husband's feelings, and declined the pension voted by the Court of Directors.

Lord Hardinge always maintained that such honours from his Queen and country more than repaid him for his previous months of exertion and anxiety. But what touched his heart more than anything else was the unanimous approval of the Cabinet, backed as it was by the sincere congratulations of all his old friends. Let me record what Sir Robert Peel wrote on the subject:—

'Whitehall Gardens, April, 1846.

'MY DEAR HARDINGE,

'I know not what I can add to the simple admiration of your conduct, military and civil, throughout the whole and every insulated part of your proceedings and policy on the banks of the Sutlej. The original forbearance, the promptitude and skill with which a scandalous and unprovoked aggression was repelled, the full reparation demanded, the dignity and calm fortitude with which it was insisted upon, the wisdom of the conditions imposed with reference not merely to our character for moderation in victory, but to the permanent interests of the Indian Empire, are themes on which volumes might be written. These volumes, however, could add nothing to the assurance of *the most cordial approbation* of every act that has been done and every line that has been written.'

A few days later Sir Robert Peel wrote again:—

'There is here universal approval and admiration of your policy *from first to last*; above all things, your moderation after victory is most applauded. It is thought, and justly thought, that it adds a lustre to the skill and valour displayed in the military achievements. It is ten times more gratifying to the public mind than the annexation of the whole of the Punjab would have been.

'This is the common sentiment, the instinctive

feeling of the whole mass of mankind; but your policy is as cordially approved by the reflecting few. They consider that the annexation of the Punjab would have been a source of weakness and not of strength, that it would have extended our frontier at the greatest distance from our resources and on the weakest points, that you would have been with reference to Afghanistan and all the bordering countries in a much worse position than you were in September last.

'These are Indian considerations; but there are higher considerations still nearer home, affecting still more vital interests, that are decisive in favour of your policy. There is not a country in Europe or America that does not do us justice, that does not admire the signal proof of bravery and military skill ten times the more, because it was called forth in a righteous cause and because it has been followed by dignified forbearance and moderation in the hour of strength. I believe that what has taken place on the banks of the Sutlej will have its influence on the banks of the Oregon; that there is not an American who will not feel that if England follows the example you have set of moderation and justice in her negotiations, and is compelled to vindicate her rights or her honour by an appeal to arms, she will also follow on the St. Lawrence or the Hudson the example of disciplined valour and heroic devotion.'

In the same month Sir R. Peel offered Lord Hardinge the Master-Generalship of the Ordnance, then on the point of being vacated. This arrangement was contingent on his deciding to return home at the close of the military operations.

Lord Ripon, President of the Board of Control, wrote in the same strain and in equally cordial language. Then came pouring in addresses from different bodies at home and in India—the City of London, the Mayor of Liverpool, the Corporations of Durham and Launceston (his former constituencies), the Council at Calcutta, public meetings of the natives of Calcutta and Madras—all eulogising his policy and praising its moderation; while there were hardly any of his old military and political friends who did not add something to the chorus of congratulations.

Peel's letter was a source of intense pleasure and satisfaction. Lord Hardinge wrote, in reply, that if his office was wanted when his old Chief went out he hoped the whole policy of the war would be scrutinised; that Peel had nobly supported him; that he was truly happy in such a vindicator of his actions and measures, and in such a friend who so honourably supported those whom he employed. On the 4th of July Peel wrote again:—'You will see that we are *out*, defeated by a combination of Whigs and Protectionists. I had the satisfaction of seeing two drowsy Masters in Chancery announce at the table that the Lords had passed the Corn Bill. I was satisfied. Two hours after we were ejected from power.' The next day the news arrived that the Oregon question was settled. Peel's two forecasts were thus verified. He had predicted in a former letter that he would drive his enemies (the Protectionists) across the Sutlej; in a later one he alluded to the policy adopted at Lahore as being not without influence on the Oregon.

Lord Hardinge was now sorely tempted to resign. Domestic reasons were for the moment uppermost in his mind; he also felt that it would not be equally pleasant to serve under those who had been politically opposed to him at home. But he came to the conclusion that, should the new Government press him, he was prepared to stay, as he felt bound to watch the issue of his recent policy in the Punjab. The Duke and Peel both urged him to remain; and on the 8th of July Lord John Russell sent him the following letter:—'I take advantage of the opportunity afforded me by coming into office to offer you my hearty congratulations on your brilliant victories and unchequered success. I am sure that no other Chief can so well consolidate the peace you have achieved as yourself. The Eastern nations obey a vigorous rule, but would easily evade all obligations if they did not fear the consequences. I trust, therefore, we shall have the advantage of your continuance in the Government of India.' The new President of the Board of Control, Sir John Hobhouse, addressed him to the same effect.

These letters removed whatever hesitation he may have felt. He replied, as a soldier should, that he was at their command. One stipulation, however, he made. Looking to the fact that he was arriving at that period of life when public servants had some claim to repose, he trusted that in the following year he might be permitted to resign the high trust which had been conferred upon him. He wrote to his wife that it was essential to the last act of his public life not to shrink from the responsibility of his Punjab policy, for the whole of that policy had been accomplished without the advice of his Council in Calcutta, and its results rested entirely on his own shoulders.

The period of repose at Simla was interrupted in October, 1846, by the news of a short-lived insurrection in Kashmír. The Shaikh Imám-ud-dín, not without the connivance of Lál Singh and possibly other members of the Sikh Darbár, at last openly refused to carry out that clause of the Treaty of Lahore by which Kashmír was to be transferred to Ghuláb Singh. Without an hour's hesitation, the Governor-General declared that the Treaty must be enforced by British troops. Eight regiments of Native infantry, with twelve field guns, were at once dispatched from the Jálandhar Doáb, accompanied by a Darbár contingent, consisting of 17,000 of those very Sikhs who had fought against us. The whole force was under the command of Brigadier Wheeler, with Henry Lawrence as Political Officer. The Sikhs behaved admirably on the march; and had the necessity arisen, no one doubted that they would have shown the same spirit on our side as in the hard-fought fields on the Sutlej.

But the Shaikh, who had at his disposal not more

than 8000 or 9000 men, saw at once that his cause was hopeless before the expedition had entered the passes leading into Kashmír. He hurried down to tender his submission in person, and proceeded to make disclosures which involved Lál Singh in his downfall. It appeared that he had long been wavering between Ghuláb Singh's offer to confirm him in his government with a salary of one lakh of rupees (£120,000 a year), and Lál Singh's bribe of a receipt in full for his past accounts. He now showed letters from Lál Singh ordering him to oppose the transfer of Kashmír.

Lál Singh was forthwith put upon his trial on the charge of having treacherously violated the Treaty of Lahore, to which his own signature had been appended. The trial took place in public, before a court of British officers, composed of Sir John Littler, Currie, the two Lawrences, and Colonel Goldie. They recorded their unanimous opinion that the charge of treachery was established. The deposition of Lál Singh was accordingly demanded. To this the other members of the Darbár gave an equally unanimous assent. The great Sikh chieftain, who had first crossed swords with us at Múdkí and Firozsháh, was now, despite the ravings of the Lahore Messalina, deported to British territory, leaving a name remarkable only for intrigues and excesses of every shade of iniquity.

It was argued at the time in some quarters that the Kashmír insurrection arose from the aversion of the

Muhammadan population to the Hindu sovereign who had been forced upon them. In reply to this, it is sufficient to quote the high authority of Henry Lawrence [1], who declared that the arrival of Ghuláb Singh in Kashmír was by no means displeasing to the inhabitants, the tyranny and oppression of the Shaikh having become insupportable.

The Kashmír insurrection and the treachery of Lál Singh led to a revision of the Treaty of Lahore, in a direction which the Governor-General had for some time been contemplating. In a despatch to the Secret Committee, dated from Simla, September 10th, 1846, after discussing the advisability of continuing the occupation of Lahore by British troops, he added: 'The other course which it may be open to the British Government to take, and which has constantly occupied my attention, would be to carry on the government of Lahore in the name of the Mahárájá during his minority, a period of about eight years, placing a British Minister at the head of the government assisted by a Native Council.

'The marked difference between the system of having a British Minister residing at Lahore conducting the government by native agency, and that which now prevails, would amount to this: that in the one case our troops are made the instruments for supporting misrule; and in the other, by British interposition, justice and moderation are secured by an

[1] See the Governor-General's despatch of November 21st, 1846, to the Secret Committee.

administration through native executive agency in accordance with the customs, feelings, and prejudices of the people. If, therefore, the proposal of the Regent and Darbár should lead to an offer to carry on the government by a British Minister, and the proposal should be confirmed by the influential chiefs, I should be disposed to give the experiment a favourable consideration.'

The contingency here contemplated had now arrived. In December, 1846, the Governor-General again visited Lahore. He announced that he was ready to withdraw the troops in accordance with the existing Treaty; but that, if the Darbár still wished for British protection, they must consent to the only conditions on which it could be afforded. Accordingly, a new Treaty was signed. The Rání was excluded from all power, receiving a pension of £15,000 a year. A Council of Regency, consisting of eight Sardárs, was appointed during the minority of Dhulíp Singh; and it was stipulated that they should act under the control and guidance of the British Resident. A British garrison was to occupy the Punjab during the same period of eight years, to be stationed in whatever towns and forts the Governor-General might think fit; while the Sikh Darbár agreed to pay £220,000 a year towards the expenses of occupation. The first Resident was Sir Henry Lawrence; and when he was compelled to take sick-leave in 1847, he was succeeded by Sir Frederic Currie, both of whom had taken a prominent part in all the preceding negotiations.

This Second Treaty of Lahore, which governed our relations with the Punjab until the outbreak at Múltán in 1848, was negotiated by Lord Hardinge on his own responsibility, without reference to his Council at Calcutta or to the Home Government. But he had been entrusted with full authority to adopt whatever policy he thought best, and he subsequently received the most cordial approval of the Treaty. This may be seen from the following letters, written at different times by Sir J. Hobhouse, President of the Board of Control.

In December, 1846, after the news of the suppression of the insurrection in Kashmír, he wrote :—'I may now congratulate you, as I do most cordially, on the success of your operations against the Shaikh. This termination of a very threatening and embarrassing affair will leave you at leisure to consider the state of affairs at Lahore, and to determine the important question of remaining in or quitting the Punjab. You are in possession of our sentiments on the subject. But let me again say that we leave the decision to you, who are on the spot with all the materials for forming a correct judgment immediately before you; and also that, do what you may, you will be supported by us.' Again, in January, 1847, 'Let me say that all you have hitherto done inspires us with the perfect confidence that all you will do will be well done.' And, finally, after the Second Treaty of Lahore had been received in England, 'I have now only to congratulate you on all you have done and are doing.

You will see by the newspapers that even the best guides of public opinion are now delighted with your arrangements, and give you credit for biding your time and doing the right thing at the right moment.'

These last words embody the principles by which Lord Hardinge was always guided in his dealings with the Punjab. His policy varied from time to time, but only with the circumstances of the case. While deliberately averse to annexation, he never disguised from himself that such a contingency might be forced upon him. A writer in the *Calcutta Review*, defending the Treaty of December 1846, thus expressed the alternative that was present to the Governor-General's mind: 'If the time arrives when the Darbár and the army grow weary of our honesty, then no voice will be louder than ours for punishing the State by complete annexation.' When that time did arrive, Lord Hardinge's voice joined in approving the policy which was forced upon his successor. In a letter from England to Sir Henry Lawrence, dated March 24th, 1849, he wrote:—'The energy and turbulent spirit of the Sikhs are stated by one section [of politicians here] as ground for *not* annexing. In my judgment, this is the argument which would dispose me, if I were on the spot, to annex. . . . I should be ashamed of myself if I would not depart from a line of policy which was right at the time, because I might be charged with inconsistency.'

CHAPTER XI

NEPÁL AND OUDH

AT this period the State of Nepál was very unsettled. The Mahárájá had proceeded to Benares on a pilgrimage, to expiate the guilt which might attach to himself and his family in consequence of the assassination of thirty-five chiefs in the Audience Hall at Khatmandu. He was accompanied by the Rání and her two children, while the heir-apparent remained behind with the Minister, Jang Bahádúr. The latter was himself deeply implicated in the murder of the chiefs, under the orders, it is alleged, of the Rání, in revenge for the assassination of her principal Minister.

These proceedings were involved in much mystery, but the following is an outline of the story as reported at the time to the Governor-General. The Minister of the Rání had been shot during his devotions. On hearing the news, the Rání hastened to the spot with her female attendants, and, taking the Sword of State in her own hands, walked on foot to the Audience Hall in the Palace. Jang Bahádúr, who was then in command of the army, observed that, as the Rání had been invested with full powers, it behoved her to make the most searching inquiry and to punish the offenders. The Mahámájá in the mean time arrived, attended by his Sardárs, with the exception of one old chief and his relations. The Rání ordered the absent chief to be brought before her, and directed another chief, suspected of being concerned in the murder, to be placed in irons, exhorting him to confess his crime. He declared his innocence, and the Rání gave her sword to the General attending upon her, and desired him to kill the suspected chief.

The Mahárájá now interfered, declaring that it would be criminal to put to death so old a servant of the State without trial. He mounted his horse and proceeded to the Residency to ask advice. In the mean time the absent chief suspected of the murder arrived with his followers, and was met by Jang Bahádúr, who related to him what had happened, and declared it was necessary, in order to appease the Rání, that the chief in irons and General Abhimán Singh should be put to death. This advice was rejected. The General, hearing of the conspiracy against him, collected his soldiers and ordered them to load. As they approached, the Rání descended from the gateway and entering the Hall with the Sword of State exclaimed, 'Who has killed my Minister? Name him quickly, or with this sword I shall kill the prisoner.' This was prevented by the chiefs placing themselves in her way. On her re-ascending the staircase, followed by General Abhimán Singh, he and the old chief were shot down.

The massacre then commenced. The troops under Jang Bahádúr fired on the chiefs, the Ráni exclaiming, 'Kill and destroy my enemies.'

Jang Bahádúr was then invested with the office of Minister. The Mahárájá reproached him with the massacre; while the Ráni broke out into loud lamentations, declaring that unless the heir-apparent were at once put to death, in order to open the succession to her own son, 'more bloodshed would follow.' Jang Bahádúr laid his turban at the feet of the Mahárájá, and begged that he might have full powers to 'remove' the enemies of the heir-apparent. He forthwith killed in cold blood the chiefs who had espoused the cause of the Ráni. She was then informed that she must quit Khatmandu, together with her sons, while the Mahárájá was also persuaded to accompany her to Benares.

The Governor-General had no right by Treaty to interfere in the internal affairs of Nepál, which then, as now, ranked as an independent state, outside the sphere of British suzerainty. All he could do was to write a letter to the Resident to the following effect:—That the previous acts of atrocity committed by the Minister, in first ordering the massacre of thirty-five chiefs in the Hall of Audience, and next in putting to death twenty-six influential chiefs, the adherents of the Rani, and thus by terror preventing the Mahárájá from returning to his capital, were reasons which induced him to be in no haste to recognise the son who, under guidance of this Minister, had supplanted his father. The Governor-General could only express his hope that some arrangement might be made between the parties before his acknowledgment of the new sovereign was demanded.

This ghastly story of intrigue and massacre in Nepál must sound almost incredible to the present generation, who only know Jang Bahádúr as the lion of a London season and the ally of England during the Mutiny. To us at the time in India it recalled the bulletins of similar proceedings which we had been accustomed to receive from Lahore before the Sikh invasion. In Eastern countries such tragedies have from time immemorial been incidental to a disputed succession. And those critics who are disposed to condemn the extension of British rule in India, should bear in mind that it has given protection not only to the population at large, but also to the native princes who still retain the administration of their own dominions.

On his way to Lucknow, where his presence was required to administer a personal rebuke to the King of Oudh for his intolerable maladministration, the Governor-General halted for a few days in the neighbourhood of the Tarái, in order to witness a tiger hunt. Although he had lost one hand he was an excellent shot, resting his gun on what remained of his left arm. The 'battue' was organised almost on military principles, the beaters consisting of no less than seventy elephants in line. A larger number may have been collected when the Prince of Wales visited

India in later years; but no one who was present on this occasion can have forgotten the strange and picturesque scene. The sagacious animals crashed through the heavy jungle, uprooting with their trunks the smaller trees in their way, and avoiding with natural instinct the dangerous bogs that abounded. The sport was excellent, two or three tigers being brought back to camp each day. The Lord Sahib was as keen as the youngest staff-officer, especially when a tiger was on foot. We all felt that he had well earned such relaxation after the constant anxieties of the last two years.

Thence we proceeded to Cawnpur, then known only as a large cantonment and a prosperous mercantile town, but destined ten years later to be the scene of that terrible tragedy with which its name must ever hereafter be associated. There we crossed the Ganges, and entered the dominions of the King of Oudh, which are naturally fertile and densely inhabited. The population especially attracted our notice, as supplying at that time the best high-caste Sepoys to the Bengal army. Lucknow, the capital, is a good specimen of an Eastern city, studded with palaces, mosques, and other picturesque buildings. When illuminated at night, as on the occasion of the Governor-General's visit, the effect was most striking. I can only speak of Lucknow as it was in 1847. The vicissitudes which it has since gone through may have changed its aspect materially; but in those days its situation on the river Gúmti, with the mosque of

Alí Masjíd overhanging it, left, from an artistic point of view, nothing to be desired.

It cannot be denied that, from the days of Lord Wellesley, maladministration had been more or less chronic in Oudh. Successive Governors-General had placed on record their solemn words of warning—words destined to be disregarded until the last crisis arrived in 1856. One of the first acts of Lord Hardinge on his arrival in India had been to protest against the displacement of the Wazír by a mere upstart, in opposition to the declared wishes of the Resident. Friendly advice was tendered on that occasion, but it remained unheeded. The year 1847 arrived, but with it no manifest improvement. It was under such circumstances that the present visit of remonstrance was undertaken.

To illustrate the unsettled state of affairs, an incident that occurred in April of this very year may be mentioned. The city of Lucknow had been much disturbed, apparently by a bad spirit among the Hindu population directed against the Musalmán authorities, in consequence of some Hindu temples having been thrown down. The King was unpopular, and even his life was in danger. When it was least expected, an armed soldier with two or three followers forced their way into the palace, where they were immediately cut down. On the day following, the Minister was attacked by four men, who struck him to the ground and held daggers at his breast, threatening his life if any attempt were made at a rescue. A crowd was formed round this group, no one venturing to interfere. On hearing of the disturbance, Colonel Richmond, the Resident, hastened to the spot, with a regiment and two guns, when the same threats were repeated. Two of these desperadoes held the Minister down, while the others succeeded in intimidating the lookers-on. These men declaimed against the bad government of the King, and demanded £5000 as the price of the Minister's life. The Resident refused to be a party to any pecuniary arrangements of that nature. He told them that, if they killed the Minister, they should answer for it with their own lives; but, on the other hand, if they spared his life, their own would be guaranteed. Lieutenant Bird, Assistant to the Resident, then forced his way into the crowd, when suddenly two elephants, carrying the required sum, came upon the scene. The money had been provided by the Minister's relations. But the troops seized the delinquents and escorted them to prison. Colonel Richmond then went to the King, to whom it was explained that, in order to save the Minister's life, he had given these men two alternatives: either to be liberated, taking their chance of escape; or to submit to a fair trial, on the understanding that their lives would not be forfeited. The King assented, and the men decided upon standing their trial.

The Governor-General expressed his displeasure that the Resident had become implicated as the protector of such ruffians, but enjoined him to observe the good faith of a British officer, and to prevent their being mutilated or treated with inhumanity, recourse to which was by no means improbable. Such was the state of the government, and such were the scenes frequently enacted in Oudh before the Governor-General's arrival in the province. They told the same tale as at Lahore and Khatmandu—pointing to two alternatives, either more direct interference by the British Government in internal affairs, or the drastic remedy of annexation.

On his arrival at the palace, the Governor-General was received with every mark of honour. Darbárs were held and the most costly presents offered, with a general illumination of the city. The King, a sensualist in appearance, seemed to be lavish to excess in all his surroundings. Entertainments were provided in our honour. These consisted mainly of fights in the arena between various kinds of wild animals—tigers, buffaloes, and hyenas contending together. Even quails were pitted against each other to provide amusement for the royal party. There he sat in his throne of state, as a Roman Emperor may have done in days gone by; but the dignity and kingly appearance was wanting. After being satiated with these sanguinary exhibitions, the Court retired, and then the serious part of the conference began. The words of warning had been carefully prepared. They were described as the 'golden' advice of the Governor-General to the King. 'Golden,' it may be presumed, because the whole was subsequently transcribed in golden letters with the most elaborate illuminations for presentation to the Governor-General.

The letter commenced by drawing the King's attention to the forbearance of the British Government and its strict observance of treaties in the case of the Punjab and Kashmír. Then it was explained how Lord Wellesley's Treaty of 1801 provided for the protection of the people, and how their rights were secured to them by the Convention of 1802. It was required of the King that he should reform the defects of his police administration, as well as those of the judicial and revenue departments. It was stated that, if oppression and misrule should continue to prevail, the Government reserved to itself the right of appointing its own officers for the administration of the country. Attention too was drawn to the sixth article of the Treaty of 1801, which enjoined the Governor-General to carry out its provisions, with reference especially to the case of the peasants. The King was reminded how Lord William Bentinck had tendered similar advice in 1831, and how he had threatened to bring the province under British rule. He was also reminded how, only three years before, he had been addressed in these terms:—'The maladministration of Oudh is extreme. Necessary arrangements must be made in reparation. I am extremely sorry that the Wazír has been obliged to resign, contrary to the wishes of the British Resident. Notwithstanding this, your Majesty has dismissed him on your accession to the throne and appointed another Minister.'

Since that date many acts of tyranny and oppression had been proved beyond all doubt. The letter proceeded:—'In case of delaying the execution of this policy, it has been determined by the Government of India to take the management of Oudh under their own authority.' Then, alluding to the King's inexperience, it further stated that the reform of such a bad system could not be expected to take effect at once. The first step would be to ascertain the rental of every estate and to fix a moderate assessment on each, so that the cultivators might know exactly their amount of taxation. This was to be effected in two years; and if the misrule had not diminished during that time, the Government would then feel justified in adopting extreme measures.

The above was the purport of the letter of warning. That it proved ineffectual may be gathered from what took place in 1854. Colonel Outram's report of that year proved that not only had no improvement taken place, but that Oudh was completely delivered over to anarchy and oppression. Thereupon Lord Dalhousie advised that, while the King should be permitted to retain his title, the whole of the administration should be transferred to officers of the Company. This was the more lenient course, but the Home Government adopted a sterner policy. The final orders for annexation were issued, and Oudh became in 1856 a British province.

CHAPTER XII

RESULTS OF ADMINISTRATION. RETURN HOME

LORD HARDINGE had devoted much of his time during his stay at Simla to the consideration of certain civil measures of administration, which were either initiated or carried to completion before he left India.

Foremost among these was the question of continuing the great scheme of irrigation known as the Ganges Canal, which had been commenced many years before, and was not opened till 1856. Up to Lord Hardinge's time the project had encountered serious opposition, notably from Mr. Thomason, then Lieutenant Governor of the North-Western Provinces; it also met with but lukewarm support in other quarters. Major Cautley, who had originated the scheme, was in England; while his assistant-engineer, Captain Baker, had been detached on military duty. On the one side, it was urged that the construction of the canal would cause such interference with the natural drainage as to produce chronic malaria. On the other side, it was alleged that the people preferred to take their chance of fever if assured of a constant water-supply. Lord Hardinge decided that, however great the risk of malaria, the dangers of probable famine were much greater. He consequently ordered the works to proceed, though irrigation was stopped near the large towns, so as to minimise the injurious consequences. The cultivators of the Doáb owe a heavy debt of gratitude to the Governor-General for his firmness in this matter. Not only has the Ganges Canal saved the country from drought and permitted the regular cultivation of more valuable crops, but it has also proved a great financial success. According to the latest returns, which have been supplied to me by high authority, more than 600,000 acres are now irrigated every year; while the profits yield a return of 5½ per cent. a year on an expenditure of nearly £3,000,000 sterling. An extension of the original scheme, called the Lower Ganges Canal, has recently been opened, with every promise of no less favourable results.

Three subjects, which strongly aroused the feelings of Lord Hardinge, may conveniently be grouped together: Human sacrifice, *satí*, and infanticide. Mention has already been made of the measures adopted, soon after his landing in India, to deal with the practice of human sacrifice among the wild tribe of Khonds in the Orissa mountains. By adding no fewer than sixteen officers to the staff already employed in that region under Major Macpherson, Lord Hardinge was able to boast that human sacrifice was practically suppressed during his term of government; nor has there since been any recrudescence of the practice.

To Lord William Bentinck belongs the credit of being the first Governor-General who prohibited *satí*, or the burning of widows on the funeral-pile of their husbands. The prohibition was necessarily confined to British territory, and the practice still continued in Native States. Two notable instances occurred at this time. On the occasion of the murder of Hira Singh at Lahore, twenty-four women sacrificed themselves, of whom four were his wives; and when the Rájá of Mandi, near Simla, died, twelve widows were burned alive with his body.

So also with female infanticide. It cannot be maintained that the crime is yet extinct among certain classes, and in certain parts of the country; but in those days it was rampant and scarcely concealed. I have myself heard the Mahárájá Dhulíp Singh describe how, when a child at Lahore, he had seen his sisters put into a sack and thrown into the river. The Governor-General did all in his power to put an end to these two kinds of crime in Native States. His procedure was first to persuade the princes to declare them illegal, and then to instruct the British Resident to see that their edicts were carried out, under pain of his extreme displeasure. At the present day, it may be said that *satí* is unknown throughout India, except perhaps in the independent State of Nepal; and that infanticide is dying out in Native States as it has died out in British territory.

The following may be cited as some of the principal improvements made during the years 1846–47:—The

Calcutta Conservancy was reformed; transit duties were abolished between Native States in Central India and on the Sutlej, that river and the Indus being now practically freed from these imposts; while the cultivation of tea was much encouraged, under the superintendence of Dr. Jameson—especially in Assam, where a company was formed for that purpose.

The preservation of the ancient monuments of India also engaged the attention of the Governor-General. He greatly admired the Táj, and ordered parts of it to be repaired, as well as the palace at Agra. He also removed the unseemly and grotesque ornament which had been placed on the top of the Kutab Minar at Delhi. Of all these celebrated buildings he caused photographs to be taken—photography then being an art almost unknown in India.

This slight sketch of what was accomplished in civil administration shows that the Governor-General had not been idle or remiss. When the charge was brought against him, that he was so immersed in warlike operations as to neglect such duties, a writer in the *Calcutta Review* called it one of those 'drizzling criticisms which he could well afford to ignore.'

As some misapprehension may exist with regard to the military reforms which Lord Hardinge carried out after the close of the Sutlej campaign, it must be noted that, on the one hand, the condition of the finances imperatively demanded that some reduction should be made in the military budget; while on the other, his experience in the field had taught him how such a reduction could be effected without any diminution in the general efficiency of the army. As an old Secretary at War, Lord Hardinge was peculiarly qualified to appreciate and to reconcile all the various considerations which entered into the problem he had to solve. The first principle that he always kept before him was to maintain unimpaired the strength of the European troops in India; the second was to redistribute the entire army, so that the North-West Frontier and the Punjab might be secured against any contingency.

Subject to these two dominant principles, Lord Hardinge now felt himself justified in disbanding no fewer than 50,000 Sepoys, and reducing the strength of the Native regiments from 1000 to 800 men[1]. Even thus, the army was more numerous than it had been in 1837, the last year of peace in India. It is true that, after the annexation of the Punjab, the former establishments were restored; but, as stated by Sir William Hunter, Lord Dalhousie afterwards became convinced of the impolicy of this increase, and himself proposed a reduction. In Madras, the Native army was reduced under Lord Hardinge by 10,000 men; and in Bombay by 7000 men. But at the same time the Native Cavalry was augmented by eight regiments; and Sindh and Sikh levies were enrolled for the frontier police, which thus assumed a semi-military

[1] These numbers appear in Sir H. Lawrence's article in the *Calcutta Review* for 1847, vol. viii. He obtained his figures from Col. Wood, then Military Secretary to the Governor-General.

character. The number of European regiments in Bombay remained the same, but some of those in Madras were transferred to the Bengal establishment. In the general result, the total European force in India was stronger by 10,000 men when Lord Hardinge resigned office than it had been in 1837; while the Bengal army alone, European and Native, was stronger by 30,000 men.

The condition of the ordnance naturally attracted a special share of Lord Hardinge's attention. The strength of the artillery, as regards both men and guns, was fully maintained. The nine-pounders (sixty in number), which had previously been drawn by bullocks, were now horsed. Measures were also adopted to place both field and siege artillery in a more satisfactory position with reference to reserves of ammunition. At Firozsháh, and again at Alíwál, the ammunition had run short. In the former battle some excuse may be made, for out of seventeen artillery waggons that went into action seven were blown up by the enemy's fire.

The result of these reductions was to effect a saving of no less that £1,160,000 in the military budget. When to this was added the Lahore subsidy of £220,000, and the revenue from the Jálandhar Doáb and Cis-Sutlej districts of about £500,000, the entire improvement in the finances amounted to £1,880,000 —a relief from financial strain such as the Indian exchequer had not enjoyed since 1838.

These reductions were more or less unpopular in

the army, as reductions always must be; but the question involved was whether the force that remained was adequate for any emergency that might arise. The strength left was not, indeed, the strength of numbers; it was the strength of a better distribution from a strategical point of view. The garrisons on the North-West Frontier had been doubled. On the Sutlej there were 50,000 men, with sixty guns; at Firozpur 10,000 men, complete in every detail; and at Lahore 9000 men. The Punjab was quiet; and when the insurrection subsequently broke out at Múltán, Lord Gough had an ample force for the operations which followed.

While dealing with questions relating to the army, I must not forget to mention the various boons conferred upon the Sepoys. As before mentioned, twelve months' 'batta' was granted to them at the end of the war; their pension for wounds was increased from four to seven rupees a month; hutting money was allowed; and all wounded men received a free ration in hospital. Lord Hardinge had been called in England the 'soldier's friend.' Might he not also be called the friend of the Sepoy?

Looking to the fact that Lord Hardinge was less than four years in India, this catalogue of work done shows what an active mind, untiring labour, and complete confidence in subordinates, can achieve. Now he was longing for his holidays, like a schoolboy. In one of the last letters which he wrote to his wife are these words:—'I must shrink from no duty to a public which has rewarded me so largely, and must maintain to the last the principle which I exact from my subordinates, that public interests ought not to be neglected. Whilst war and bankruptcy threatened the State, I remained. Now, that peace is established and prosperity reviving, I return with the consciousness that I have done my duty.'

It is well to record, in these last days of his administration, the debt of obligation he felt to those officers who had served him so faithfully during the intricate details and difficult negotiations of his Punjab policy. Many of these 'politicals' were soldiers by profession, who, when the war broke out, aided him either in the field or in the districts where the presence of military men was required to inspire confidence. They were a goodly list :—Henry and George Lawrence, Broadfoot, the four Abbotts, Benson, the Bechers, Lake, Reynell Taylor, Robert Napier, and last (not least) Herbert Edwardes. All these have made their mark in the annals of Indian history. By their side may be ranged the civilians, such as John Lawrence, Currie, Elliot, Maddock, Dorin, Cust, W. Edwards, and a host of others.

As the services of many of these distinguished men have been dealt with in formal biographies, I need not enlarge on their merits. One word, however, must be said as to the services of the two brothers so intimately connected with Punjab administration. Nor can I forget, amid the host of Indian worthies of that period, the name of George Broadfoot. He was the right-hand man of the Governor-General in the earlier days of the Sikh negotiations, and to him Lord Hardinge owed especial acknowledgments. It has been whispered that Broadfoot's instincts were too aggressive, but there is no evidence to show that this was the case. Had he developed any such tendency, it would assuredly have been detected. The Governor-General on all occasions confided in him, and both at home and in India Broadfoot received due acknowledgment for his unremitting zeal and constant exertions.

Henry Lawrence had been unknown to Lord Hardinge, except by reputation. It was not until he was hastily summoned from Nepál to the seat of war that his character and qualities shone forth. Charming and amiable, with strong religious feelings, he was conscientious to a degree in his views and principles. His resignation of his seat at the Lahore Board, when those principles seemed to be involved, and his withdrawal of his resignation from a sense of public duty, are matters of history. It has been truly said that to know Henry Lawrence was to love him. He accompanied Lord Hardinge to England, and constant intercourse during a long sea voyage served only to bring out those qualities which he had so often extolled. It is related that, when Henry Lawrence left Lahore to take up his new appointment in Rájputána, there was hardly a dry eye among the host of friends, European and native, who came to bid him farewell.

John Lawrence, the future 'Ruler of India,' was a

man whose character was cast in a different mould from that of his brother. At the time of the progress of the Governor-General up the country in 1845, he was magistrate at Delhi, being known even then as a civilian of no ordinary ability. Lord Hardinge at once fixed his eye on him. He had been unusually active in forwarding stores and supplies to the Frontier, so that when his services on the Sutlej were applied for, Mr. Thomason demurred to losing so good an officer. On the close of the war he was immediately selected to take charge of the Jálandhar Doáb, which had now become a British province. The Governor-General entertained so high an opinion of his services that one of his last acts, as recorded in Mr. Bosworth Smith's biography, was to recommend him for one of the high appointments then about to become vacant. John Lawrence's later career is now a chapter in the history of India, as eventful as it is honourable in every way to his memory.

The names of Hardinge and Gough must always be connected with the battle-fields of the Sutlej. The two chiefs had sometimes differed—differed too on important tactical and strategical questions; but such was the mutual good-fellowship between them that their differences were soon merged in the single desire of bringing matters to a successful issue. As Lord Hardinge wrote in a semi-official letter shortly before he sailed for England:—'The energy and intrepidity of the Commander-in-Chief, Lord Gough, and his readiness to carry on the service in cordial co-operation with the Governor-General, have overcome many serious obstacles.' Their complete unanimity on the night of the 21st of December, as well as in the plan of attack at Sobráon, is an instance showing how any want of such co-operation might have led to deplorable results. Again, in a letter written to a friend from Simla in May, 1846, Lord Hardinge remarks: 'I am most gratified that my excellent and distinguished friend the Commander-in-Chief has received the honours he has so nobly won. He is a fine specimen of an English officer and an English gentleman.' The two soldiers were always on friendly terms, and these relations continued till Lord Hardinge's death.

The Governor-General was now on his way to Calcutta, the seat of government which he had quitted three years before with very different feelings. Then, the state of the Punjab was a source of extreme anxiety; now, its prospects were peaceful. The captured Sikh guns, 256 in number, had already been conveyed in triumph through the country, deeply impressing the native population with a sense of our military power and inexhaustible resources.

On the 24th of December, 1847, after Lord Hardinge's arrival in Calcutta, the European and native inhabitants of the Presidency approached him in the following terms:—

'The inhabitants of Calcutta addressed your Lordship on the occasion of your return to the Presidency, and declared their sense of the distinguished services rendered by you to this country. In acknowledging that address, your Lordship expressed your conviction that a pacific course was the one best calculated to promote the honour and interests of Great Britain and the welfare of the people of India. We feel that in this belief your Lordship commenced your administration, and that it influenced you until war became the necessity of self-defence. We can desire no happier future for England and India than that this sentiment should prevail with our rulers, and no more glorious achievements when forced into the field than those which under divine Providence have won imperishable honour for our arms on the banks of the Sutlej. We cannot permit your Lordship to lay down the high office of Governor-General without the expression of our admiration for your distinguished career. We desire to have and preserve in Calcutta some personal memorial of one who has received the highest honours from the Sovereign and the thanks of his countrymen whilst ruling this vast empire.'

The result of this address was the erection of the statue by J. H. Foley, R.A., previously referred to. It was pronounced by the Royal Academy to be admirable as a work of art; and none could better befit the character and services of the man.

The salutes which announced the arrival of Lord Dalhousie in the Húglí were indeed welcome sounds. Then followed the same interchange of ceremonials, with their attendant hospitalities, in which Lord Hardinge had been the principal actor a few years previously. Now, passing through the line of troops, the slim figure and handsome countenance of India's 'new Ruler' was narrowly scanned by the crowd that surrounded the steps of Government House. The short period that intervened between the arrival of the new Governor-General and the departure of his predecessor afforded an opportunity for an interchange of views on those questions which pressed for consideration. Their discussions led to a satisfactory concurrence of opinion, and the two statesmen parted with that confidence in each other which their antecedents inspired.

On the 18th of January, 1848, Lord Hardinge, with Henry Lawrence and his personal staff, embarked on the 'Mozuffer,' a war steamer of the East India Company. Crowds witnessed his departure. There were interesting passengers—a tiger and Himalayan pheasants for the Queen; Chinese dogs, and the old charger Miáni, who came home to end his days in England. Once beyond the Sandheads a prosperous run was made to Aden, where Lord Hardinge landed, revisiting the works and making his final report on the defences of the rock.

In view of the contingency of military operations in Egypt at any future time, Lord Hardinge had been directed by the Home Government to report on the character of the route between Kosseir, on the Red Sea, and the Nile. Mehemet Ali, then absent from Egypt on account of his health, afforded us every facility. On our landing, tents and all the apparatus of Eastern travel were found ready for our march. The route taken was that which had been chosen by Sir D. Baird when he landed there with an Indian contingent in 1801; and it has been more than once made use of recently during the British occupation of Egypt. Some five or six days' march through a wild and rocky gorge brought us to the Nile. The soil was hard and capable of bearing guns and wheeled carriages, although, from the narrowness of the pass, this route had some disadvantages from a military point of view. On reaching the river, we were met by the present Sir C. Murray, then Consul-General, who had been deputed by the Pasha to escort us. The days passed away pleasantly, so that on our return to our old quarters at Alexandria we felt that the duty of reporting on this military route had been combined with recollections by no means uninteresting.

After a few days' repose, H. M.'s ship 'Sidon' got up steam, and on the 28th of February we were sailing up the Adriatic on a short visit to Corfu, where Lord Hardinge saw his old friend Lord Seaton, separated however by a distance of some 200 yards in consequence of our being in quarantine. Then, after a heavy gale, we were in four days safely harboured in the port of Trieste. Without an hour's delay, the journey was resumed by road and rail. We had intended to pass through Paris, but the fall of the Orleans dynasty rendered it necessary to take another route. After a week's incessant travelling night and day we reached Ostend, and embarking in a miserable cockle-shell of a steamer were delighted to find ourselves off the Tower Stairs by daybreak on the 20th of March.

The Indian career of Lord Hardinge had now closed. His measures had been characterised by moderation and vigour, and he had bequeathed to his successors an excess of income over expenditure and the probabilities of a continuance of peace. It was, perhaps, hardly to be expected that treacherous intrigues would never again disturb the existing aspect of security. But he was conscious that he had done his duty, and now looked forward to that repose which he had so long desired. In this hope he was disappointed. It has been truly said that a public man is a nation's property, and he was again destined to serve his country in that branch of the service to which he was so devotedly attached.

CHAPTER XIII

ARMY ADMINISTRATION. CONCLUSION

IN 1848, the very year of his return to England, Lord Hardinge was sent to Ireland on special duty. The Smith O'Brien riots were then agitating the country; and the Government considered that he possessed no ordinary qualifications, both civil and military, for dealing with such a crisis as might at any moment arise. On his arrival, he immediately visited the disturbed provinces; but his personal intervention was not required. The ignominious capture of the author of these riots prevented any further agitation, and Lord Hardinge returned to England.

In 1852 he was again called upon to serve in his old department of the Ordnance, a department which had brought him into public notice shortly after his first election to Parliament. His devotion to and confidence in Peel induced him to adhere to the fiscal policy which the latter had carried out in the face of the opposition of a powerful section of the Tory party. He had also voted for the repeal of the Navigation Laws, though taking no prominent part in the parliamentary struggles of that period. His political attitude was essentially Conservative on all questions not involving the principle of Free Trade, as the following correspondence will show.

'St. James' Square,

'*Feb.* 23, 1852.

'MY DEAR HARDINGE,

'Though we have not been acting as members of the same party, yet your personal kindness has been always such, and I have such a reliance upon your sense of what is due to the public interests, that having felt it my duty to take any responsibility rather than leave the Queen without a Government, and having therefore accepted office, I hope I may rely with confidence upon your giving me your valuable military assistance by accepting the office of Master-General of the Ordnance—a post which just now requires the services of our ablest administrator. I have named my intention to the Queen; and I am sure, should you accept it, the public voice will ratify the selection. I cannot imagine to myself any political question which need raise the slightest difficulty. I shall hope, therefore, to receive an early and satisfactory answer.

'Yours sincerely,

'DERBY.'

The following was the reply:—

'*23rd Feb.*, 1852.

'MY DEAR LORD DERBY,

'I came home late, and have this instant received your very kind letter. I can truly assure you that on grounds of personal regard to you, and of professional duty to the public service, I should be most anxious to afford to your Government any assistance in my power. I have, however, on every occasion since I came from India recorded my vote in favour of Free Trade measures, and in honour and consistency I cannot depart from the line I have adopted. In other respects, I believe there is no difference of opinion between us. I therefore infer that my acceptance of the office of Master-General is limited to the military administration of that department, without requiring from me any change of political opinion. If this be so, I am ready, as a professional man, to give you any assistance in my power. But if this arrangement is inconvenient to you, I shall consider the communication as strictly confidential between us, and to be treated as if it had never been made.'

In order to complete the correspondence, I must quote from Lord Derby's reply, dated Feb. 24th, 1852:—'You have rightly interpreted my abstaining from offering you the Cabinet. I wish to have you free; and though I could not offer so important an office to a political opponent, yet I hope I may rely on your neutrality if a question should arise relating to Free Trade in which you cannot concur with my views. I may add that any vote of the kind is very little likely to arise during the present session.'

It is needless to say that on these terms Lord Hardinge undertook the duties of the office. Such an understanding has seldom been arrived at in the distribution of public appointments of great importance. It shows how marked was the confidence which Lord Hardinge enjoyed, and it may be said to reflect credit on both the parties concerned.

One of the first acts of his Ordnance administration was to augment the field batteries of artillery. In his evidence before the Sebastopol Committee in May, 1855, he stated that on coming into office he had found only about forty or fifty guns fit for service in Great Britain, and those of the date of Waterloo. He at once proposed to Lord Derby's Government that 300 guns and 200 ammunition waggons should be immediately prepared. The Government assented, and the estimated sum was voted by the succeeding administration. This timely action enabled the Ordnance Department to supply seventy-eight field guns for the Crimea, which would not have been possible if the establishment had been maintained at the figure at which Lord Hardinge found it when he came into office. During the Crimean War the Ordnance was also required to send suddenly a number of heavy guns to Sebastopol. Three complete siege trains were despatched with their ammunition, proving that the department was equal to the emergency. When asked by the Committee whether the arrangements were good and the guns well manned on their arrival, he stated that according to the latest reports nothing could be more satisfactory than the state of the artillery, which presented a strong contrast to that of the French.

Lord Hardinge's services at the Ordnance were not destined to be of long duration. Later in the same year (1852), on the death of the Duke of Wellington, he was selected to succeed his old chief in the command of the army. The nomination was conveyed to him in the most flattering manner by Lord Derby. The office was one most congenial to his spirit, but he felt that he had no easy task in following so preeminent a man. Lord Raglan succeeded him at the Ordnance, remaining in that office until he took command of the army in the Crimea.

One of Lord Hardinge's first acts as Commander-in-Chief was to form a temporary camp of exercise at Chobham (July, 1853), under the command of Lord Seaton. The success of this experiment encouraged him to press on the Government the purchase of land at Aldershot for a permanent camp. Looking to the fact that nearly every nation on the Continent had established such camps of exercise, he felt that the days of simple barrack-yard drill were numbered, and that every means should be taken to render the army more efficient in field manœuvres. With this view, and considering the enclosed character of the country generally, it was necessary to secure a large tract of land for tactical purposes. He proposed in the first instance that about 9000 acres should be purchased. Lord Palmerston, then at the Home Office, entirely approved, and wrote that he would urge Lord Aberdeen and Sidney Herbert to support the proposal. The land was purchased; and we have since been in possession of a training ground for our army at Aldershot, with all its accompanying advantages, which cannot be over-estimated.

Perhaps the most important military reform with which Lord Hardinge's name is associated was the introduction into the service of the rifle, in substitution for the old smooth-bore or Brown Bess. The Small-Arms Committee of 1852, which had been appointed by his predecessor at the Ordnance, Lord Anglesey, while strongly advocating the merits of the Minie rifle, recommended that the bore should be reduced. As the result of elaborate experiments, the Enfield rifle of 1853 was finally adopted, though it is interesting to record that, even at this early date, Lord Hardinge expressed his opinion that the best rifle he had seen was a breech-loader of Mr. Prince's. The Enfield was stronger, and at the same time weighed less, than the Minie; and was then, undoubtedly, the best weapon available. It was well tested at Alma and Inkerman; in the trenches too, it was noticed that the Russians always retired more quickly when attacked with the rifle[1]. Unfortunately, as must happen at a period of transition, the rifles issued belonged to two different patterns, requiring different kinds of ammunition; while many regiments retained the old smooth-bore during the early months of the war. It was impossible to manufacture in time a sufficient number of rifles for the whole army

[1] In the words of Dr. W. H. Russell, the *Times* correspondent, 'It smote the enemy like a destroying angel.'

in the Crimea, though Liége received a large contract as well as Birmingham.

Consequent upon the adoption of the rifle, the School of Musketry at Hythe was established in 1854, under the command of Colonel Hay, for the training of instructors in musketry. One of the first officers appointed to Hythe was Captain Lane Fox, of the Grenadier Guards (now General Pitt-Rivers), whose researches in the history of firearms had been of great value to the Committee of 1852. He drew up a code of instructions in musketry, which forms the basis of the existing regulations; and he also trained the regiments to which the earliest Minie rifles had been issued, at Malta and afterwards in the Crimea. On being invalided home, he was succeeded by Colonel A. Gordon.

Since those days the art of rifle shooting has advanced by leaps and bounds, in a great measure under the stimulus furnished by the Volunteer movement, while many successive committees have conducted experiments and made reports upon every description of rifle. But the words of Lord Herbert, given in evidence before the Parliamentary Committee on Military Organisation, are not to be gainsaid:—'Lord Hardinge was the man to whom the army owes most for the improvement of weapons of war, and for carrying out those changes with the greatest energy and determination.' Nor was his attention confined to small-arms. The rifling of field and heavy guns demanded an equal share of his time.

He was continually in correspondence with the three great gunnery firms—Lancaster, Whitworth, and Armstrong—to each of whose systems he gave an impartial hearing, though none was approved for adoption in the service during his lifetime.

It is now necessary to note the purport of Lord Hardinge's general evidence before the Sebastopol Committee, presided over by Mr. Roebuck, as some might lay at his door to a certain extent the shortcomings of our military administration during the Crimean War. His position was that of every Commander-in-Chief when an army is sent abroad on active service. He was of course not responsible for the policy of the war, nor was he responsible for the results of the operations. In reply to the Committee for a detailed statement of his duties as Commander-in-Chief, he said that he was responsible for the discipline of the army; that he merely recommended officers for regimental and staff situations, while all first appointments were made by him subject to the Queen's pleasure. He also stated that he had given to Lord Raglan the selection for all the appointments in the Crimean army as they became vacant, although these appointments theoretically rested upon his own recommendation, this being done on the principle that a General in the field should select his own officers. He entirely approved of the Letter of Service, by which Lord Raglan was authorised to correspond directly with the Secretary at War, and was of opinion that the practice should be followed on all similar occasions. This Letter of Service was the same as that sent to Sir Arthur Wellesley in 1809, and again in 1815, when he took command of the army before Waterloo. As an indirect example of its advantages, Lord Hardinge mentioned that, after the landing in the Crimea, he had given his opinion to the Duke of Newcastle, but not to Lord Raglan, that the spot chosen was too close to Sebastopol.

He was then asked whether he concurred with the Duke of Newcastle in thinking that the line of demarcation between the Minister for War and the Commander-in-Chief was not inconveniently indefinite. He replied:—'I must say that, during the whole course of my transacting business with the Duke of Newcastle, I am not aware since the war broke out of any portion of the duties between us having been personally unsatisfactory, nor do I know to what the question alludes.' He subsequently said the same as regarded Lord Panmure. The real fact is that the Secretary of State has unlimited authority over the Horse Guards. 'If I were,' he said, 'to recommend an officer to go to the Crimea, and the Secretary at War thought for any reason that he was a person not fit for the post, I should at once give way or request him to send me a list of the best men he could find for my recommendation, as the ultimate appointment rested with the Secretary of State.' If any inconvenience had ever arisen, it was owing to the Secretary of State not expressing his pleasure to the Commander-in-Chief. The Secretary of State did not submit the names to the

Queen, and he did not see what advantage would accrue to him from having that power. He was a political official serving in the Cabinet, and it would matter little to him that the army should know whether it was the Duke of Newcastle or Lord Panmure who made the appointments. But to the Commander-in-Chief of the day it was of great importance that he should keep up that kind of connexion between himself and the Crown, so that the officers might know that the appointments proceeded in a certain degree upon the recommendation of the Commander-in-Chief, a privilege which had existed for the last 100 or 200 years.

He acknowledged his responsibility for advising the establishment of proper means of transport for the army, the medical arrangements, and the equipment. But with an army in the field, the commander of that army would call upon the Commissariat to furnish all transport, as the Commander-in-Chief at home would know nothing of the arrangements, which could only be made on the spot. He stated, moreover, that instructions with regard to stores for every branch of the army in the field were contained in the orders issued by the Treasury to the Commissariat Department.

With reference to equipment, military stores, &c., he remarked that ample provision had been made when the army left England. When asked whether the duty of providing general hospitals devolved on the authorities in the War Office, he said: 'Certainly'; that he himself had no power to spend a pound, all such arrangements being invariably made by the Secretary of State and not by the Commander-in-Chief. He also stated that all he could do was to give instructions to the regimental surgeons, but that when once war broke out he had nothing to say to medical arrangements beyond giving these necessary instructions. With reference to the establishment of the hospitals at Gallipoli, he could not interfere, the whole being under the control of Lord Raglan and the Minister for War in this country.

As regards clothing for the troops, when Dr. Smith advocated that the shako should be laid aside and a lighter serge frock issued, Lord Hardinge was able to say that he had already anticipated both proposals. A common blouse, as well as white cap-covers, was provided; and last, not least, the old stiff stock was abolished. More than a sufficient supply of blankets had also been sent out, with every article of field equipment. As to stoppages of pay, which had been enforced in the Crimea, even when the meat was of bad quality or insufficient, such a proceeding seemed to him to be most unjust. He quoted an instance of this which had occurred after the battle of Talavera. He had himself represented to the Duke of Wellington the discontented state of the men owing to these stoppages. The Duke said, 'I will put that right in five minutes,' and wrote an order at once to the effect that the men must have full pay when they got into quarters, and no stoppages.

It was suggested by the Committee that the Commissariat were to blame when, after supplying food for the whole army, they were suddenly called upon to provide huts and other articles, and failed to do so. Lord Hardinge said he thought not. The difficulties of the climate, the state of the roads, and, above all, the misfortune of a large army depending entirely upon the sea for its communications, made it almost beyond human effort to get things right. He maintained that no expedition ever left England under greater advantages; in the Peninsula they had no tents until 1814, four years after the Duke of Wellington assumed the command. The Commissariat animals had been allowed to dwindle down to too low a strength, the result of making war upon a peace establishment. When he himself crossed the Sutlej with 20,000 British and Native troops, his Commissariat transport consisted of no less than 120,000 baggage-animals, which had been procured without any great pressure or hardship upon the Native population.

When questioned concerning the recruits sent out to reinforce the army before Sebastopol, he gave the following explanation:—The necessity arose entirely from the fact that the peace establishment stood at so low a figure [1] that, after the first effort had been made

[1] The Commander-in-Chief has no control over the numbers of the army, which are fixed by the Secretary of War, on the authority of the Cabinet, and are included in the first vote of the Army Estimates, as annually sanctioned by Parliament.

to despatch a force of 25,000 men, no reserve of seasoned soldiers remained at home, and no means existed of supplying the waste of the army in the field except by sending out recruits. Comparing the condition of the army in the Crimea with that of the army in the Peninsula, he pointed out that, when Wellington commenced his campaign in 1808, a system of double battalions had been maintained for several years, while the militia was in a state of high efficiency, having been embodied to resist invasion. In the Crimea it was impossible to expect the same efficiency from boys, who suffered severely from the inclemency of the weather and from hard work in the trenches. He did not consider that an earlier embodiment of the militia would have made any material difference; for in the militia, too, there was at that time a very large proportion of boys. Ten battalions of the line had been brought home from the Colonies; but, before they could be utilised in the Crimea, it was necessary in some cases to fill up their ranks with recruits. These were trained as rapidly as possible, but the Cape regiments and a battalion of Rifles had a large proportion of recruits in the ranks. Their defect did not consist in being untrained, but in being under twenty years of age, and therefore unfit to bear the hard work and privations of the campaign. The root of the whole matter lay in the fact that we possessed no reserve, and no second battalions to feed the battalions in the field as had been the case in former wars. The Government entered upon the war with too low an establishment, and the strain upon the different departments proved that they were unequal to the emergency.

One of the immediate results of the Sebastopol Committee was the abolition of the Board of Ordnance as an independent department, and the transfer of all its duties and powers to the War Office, under the Secretary of State. This was effected by Letters Patent dated May 25th, 1855, confirmed by Act of Parliament (18 and 19 Vict., cap. 117). As a former Master-General, Lord Hardinge could hardly be expected to look upon this reform with unmixed feelings. He always maintained that the consolidated departments would be too cumbrous for efficiency, and that the change would never have been made if it had not been for the shortcomings in the Crimea—shortcomings which could be traced to other causes. But with characteristic loyalty, he did everything in his power as Commander-in-Chief to make the new system work well. His relations with Lord Panmure (who had succeeded the Duke of Newcastle as War Minister in February, 1855) were always cordial. Only on one occasion did any difference arise between them; and this was on a question connected with rifles, as to which Lord Panmure imagined that Lord Hardinge had exceeded his powers. A friendly correspondence ensued, and Lord Panmure ultimately admitted that he was quite mistaken.

In the previous year (1854), Lord Grey had raised an important debate in the House of Lords upon the anomaly of dividing the management of the army between three departments—the War Office, the Ordnance, and the Horse Guards. The Duke of Newcastle, then Minister for War and the Colonies, defended in the main the existing system, while Lord Panmure urged the desirability of placing the entire administration of the army under the Secretary of State, and on preserving the office of Commander-in-Chief. On this occasion, Lord Hardinge expressed himself very strongly against the creation of anything like a Board:—'If the legislature attempted to limit too much the authority and power of the Commander-in-Chief as regards the management of the troops, they would shake his authority in such a manner as to produce great difficulties in the event of our having to carry on a war.' Now that the question has again been canvassed, it seems desirable to recall the opinion of one who possessed the unique experience of having held in succession the three offices of Secretary at War, Master-General, and Commander-in-Chief.

It was during his period of office at the Horse Guards that the Militia Bill was introduced. Lord John Russell had been defeated in the Commons on the question whether the Militia should be of a general or a local character. Lord Derby came into power, and Mr. S. H. Walpole introduced his Militia Bill, which forms the basis of our present organisation. Lord Hardinge was naturally consulted on all the details. During the French War he had had opportunities of seeing how the ballot (or system of militia-recruiting by drawing lots) worked; and he came to the conclusion that, so long as the practice of purchasing substitutes was permitted, the physique of the men suffered. Although the ballot might be a powerful engine for raising the force to the required numerical standard, he argued that the militia must rest either upon a system of voluntary enlistment or upon the ballot *pur et simple*, without substitutes. Mr. Walpole's Bill was carried; and although the number of the militia still falls considerably short of its established strength, voluntary enlistment has so far succeeded that we now possess a force which is as efficient as a militia can be in time of peace, and which recent reforms have much improved.

To Lord Hardinge belongs the credit of having established the artillery branch of the militia. The Royal Artillerymen of that day threw cold water on the scheme. They contended that, with the limited amount of drill which was inherent in the militia system, it would be impossible to raise the men to the necessary standard of efficiency. Lord Hardinge was firm, and insisted on the experiment being tried. The result has undoubtedly been successful. The officers and men entered upon their new duties with zeal and energy; and we now possess a considerable force of artillerymen in the militia whose services in time of war would be invaluable for coast defence, thereby freeing the Royal Artillery for service in the field.

During the Crimean War the militia was embodied.

The regiments that volunteered for the Mediterranean were sent to garrison Malta, Gibraltar, and the Ionian Islands, while the force generally gave its due proportion of recruits to the line as long as the war lasted. The artillery militia had already attained so high a degree of efficiency that Lord Herbert proposed to incorporate the Tipperary Artillery, commanded by the late Lord Donoughmore, with the Royal Artillery. It was obvious, however, that this would injuriously affect the position of the officers of the Royal Artillery, who had qualified themselves by a long course of training and service; and the proposal dropped.

Lord Hardinge also introduced in 1856 the system of Depôt Battalions for recruiting, which have since been superseded by the Brigade Depôts, on the completion of Lord Cardwell's scheme of military re-organisation. He did not live to see the inauguration of the Volunteer movement; but, considering the views he entertained, that a soldier must shoot as well as fight, it is certain that there would have been no more ardent advocate of that powerful defensive reserve of which the country is now so proud. Another regulation which he carried was that of granting Queen's A.D.C.-ships to officers of the East India Company's service. This was prior to the amalgamation of the Indian with the Royal army. It was an honour much valued by those officers, who had hitherto been debarred as Company officers from participation in such a privilege.

The more prominent points of Lord Hardinge's military administration have now been briefly touched upon, all questions of controversy being avoided with regard to the policy and conduct of the war in the Crimea. The full history of that war has yet to be written. But enough has, I think, been stated to show that during the time he was at the Ordnance and at the Horse Guards he left his mark on the administration of both departments.

On October 18th, 1855, shortly after the fall of Sebastopol, Lord Hardinge was raised to the rank of Field-Marshal for his long and meritorious services—services which he rendered almost to the last, until he was compelled by illness to resign a command in which he took unflagging interest, only terminated by his death. He was taken ill at Aldershot in the act of presenting to the Queen the report of the Chelsea Commission of General Officers. He recovered sufficiently to be able to ride about his woods at South Park, devoting himself to those country occupations in which he took so keen an interest. A strong love for the arts [1] and for his garden was inherent in his nature—tastes often cultivated by those whose life has been passed amid scenes of anxiety, with mental and bodily toil. He passed

[1] A good water-colour artist himself, Lord Hardinge took great delight in the society of artists, being on intimate terms of friendship with Sir Francis Grant and Sir Edwin Landseer, both of whom painted pictures for him. The original of the portrait that forms the frontispiece to this volume is considered one of Grant's happiest efforts.

quietly away on the 23rd of September, 1856, in the seventy-second year of his age.

His remains lie in the quiet and picturesque churchyard of Fordcombe Church, near Penshurst, a church to the erection of which he had largely contributed as a thank-offering for many mercies. His funeral was of the most simple character, in strict accordance with his wishes. The body was carried to the grave by his own labourers. Lords Gough and Ellenborough stood by the coffin, on which were laid, as the only marks of his rank, his head-dress and the sword of Napoleon which had been given to him by the Great Duke.

A monument in Penshurst Church incorporates the following General Order, which was issued to the army on the 2nd October, 1856:—

'The Queen has a high and grateful sense of Lord Hardinge's valuable and unremitting services, and in his death deplores the loss of a true and devoted friend. No sovereign ever possessed a more honest and faithful councillor, or a more loyal, fearless, and devoted servant.'

Can any subject desire a more touching or a more honourable epitaph?

INDEX

THE END.